Robert Pęczkowski

Colour illustrati[...]
Artur J[...]

Dougl[...] SBD DAUNTLESS

STRATUS

Published in Poland in 2007
by STRATUS s.c.
Po. Box 123,
27-600 Sandomierz 1, Poland
e-mail:office@mmpbooks.biz
for
Mushroom Model Publications,
36 Ver Road, Redbourn,
AL3 7PE, UK.
e-mail: rogerw@mmpbooks.biz

http://www.mmpbooks.biz

ISBN
978-8389450-39-5

Editor in chief
Roger Wallsgrove

Editorial Team
Bartłomiej Belcarz
Artur Juszczak
James Kightly
Robert Pęczkowski

Colour Drawings
Artur Juszczak

Scale Plans
Dariusz Karnas

DTP
Robert Pęczkowski

Printed by:
Drukarnia Diecezjalna,
ul. Żeromskiego 4,
27-600 Sandomierz
tel. +48 (15) 832 31 92;
fax +48 (15) 832 77 87
www.wds.pl marketing@wds.pl

PRINTED IN POLAND

Contents

Get in the picture!
Do you have photographs of historical aircraft, airfields in action, or original and unusual stories to tell?
MMP would like to hear from you! We welcome previously unpublished material that will help to make MMP books the best of their kind. We will return original photos to you and provide full credit for your images. Contact us before sending us any valuable material: rogerw@mmpbooks.biz

Acknowledgements

I would like to thank the following people for their help and encouragement during the preparation of this publication.

Art Lochte - USA; Germán Lüer - Chile; Santiago A. Flores - Mexico; Jarosław Garlicki - Poland; Gerald W. Thomas, Air Group 4 - USA; James Kightly - Australia; Jose Fernandez - France; Malcolm Laird - New Zealand. Many Souffan - France.

On the title page:
A pair of SBDs over a carrier.

The Beginnings

In 1934 the Bureau of Aeronautics and the US Navy asked American aircraft companies to tender for a new carrier-borne scout bomber. At the same time competition was also announced for new carrier-borne fighter and torpedo aircraft.

The new aircraft would enter service on new aircraft-carriers of the US Navy, USS *Yorktown*, *Enterprise*, *Wasp*, *Hornet*, as well as *Lexington*, *Saratoga*, and *Ranger* already in use.

Designs for the new scout bomber were placed by Brewster, Curtiss, Great Lakes, Grumman, Northrop and Vought. The initial competition was not going to be won by just one design. The Navy required development of several selected designs, ordering small batches of each aircraft. Then by competitive testing and elimination, only one, the best aircraft type, would be left.

Orders were placed with Curtiss for the SBC-3 Helldiver, Brewster for the XSBA-1 (later built as the NAF SBN), Northrop for the XBT-1 and Vought for the XSB2U-1, later built as the SB2U Vindicator.

Edward A. Heinemann was given control of the development work on the Northrop Aircraft Company XBT-1 prototype, which received the Bureau of Aeronautics number BuNo 9745.

In terms of design the XBT-1 was a follow-on to the Gamma 2C and Gamma 2F, which used multi-bay wings, perfectly suited for a dive bomber. But the wings had one fault from the aircraft-carrier operation viewpoint: they could not be folded for parking in the cramped carrier environment. To solve the problem Heinemann designed the wing with an unfolded span that fitted US aircraft-carrier hangars. The span was thus 41 ft 6 in (12.65 m). The wings featured split flaps that could also be used as air brakes in dive and the XBT-1 also used the undercarriage from the Gamma 2F. The prototype was powered by the 700 hp Pratt & Whitney R-1536-66 Twin Wasp Junior. First flight was made on 19 August 1935. Unfortunately, with this engine the aircraft attained a maximum speed of only 296 km/h. Fitted with a more powerful (825 hp) R-1535-95 engine, the top speed rose to 194 knots (341 km/h). The aircraft could carry 1,000 lb of bombs to an altitude of 22,500 ft (8850 m).

XBT-1, 97-45, just after engine modification with short chord cowl. Tail fin and rudder still showed the original configuration. April 1936.

Stratus coll.

Two photos of BT-1 of VB-5
McDonnell Douglas.

Prototype trials proved that the aircraft was prone to buffeting in the dive, so it was decided to use perforated flaps, recently developed by NACA. This eliminated the buffeting and had a positive effect on the diving speed, without any adverse effect on the wings in horizontal flight.

In December 1935 the prototype was handed over for further testing by the US Navy at Naval Air Station (NAS) Anacostia.

On 18 September 1936 the US Navy ordered 54 production aircraft, under the designation BT-1.

The aircraft received US Navy BuNos. 0590-0626 and 0628-0643. The BT-1 was heavier than the prototype and it featured an altered, shorter engine cowling and enlarged vertical tail.

Operation of production BT-1s encountered many problems. The aircraft was laterally unstable in low speed flight, and aileron effectiveness was poor. Rapid increase of engine revs caused the aircraft to violently bank. These problems resulted in a number of tragic crashes. Some 39 BT-1s were used, and the US Navy failed to expand the order, quickly withdrawing the aircraft from service.

Northrop XBT-2 (Douglas XSBD-1)

Problems with flying characteristics of the BT-1 forced Heinemann to introduce some radical changes in the design. These were introduced in the prototype designated the XBT-2 (BuNo 0627). A new engine, the Wright XR-1820-32 Cyclone, was used, driving a three-blade propeller. Instrument panels and cockpit were also altered.

Early in 1937 the Northrop plant at El Segundo fell in serious financial trouble. As a result, it was taken over by Douglas Aircraft, officially on 5 April 1937. The name of the plant was thus changed to El Segundo Division of Douglas.

Jack Northrop left El Segundo on 1 January 1938 to establish a new company of his own: Northrop Aircraft Inc. based at Hawthorne, California.

First flying trials of the XBT-2 prototype commenced on 25 April 1938, but the results were not satisfactory, as the aircraft's behaviour in flight was virtually the same as that of the BT-1.

To save the design, its designer decided to test the aircraft in a wind-tunnel. The tests were carried out in the only suitable tunnel, at the NACA Langley Memorial Aeronautical Laboratory, Virginia. Tunnel-testing of the XSBD-1 prototype (the name was changed after the plant was taken over by Douglas) suggested introduction of the following changes: replace the Gamma 2F undercarriage with a completely retractable one, introduce fixed slats on the wings in order to improve aileron effectiveness, and enlarge the horizontal and vertical tail. All the changes were introduced, including a retractable undercarriage similar to that used in the A-17A. The modified XSBD-1 prototype was approved by the US Navy in February 1939 as the pattern for production aircraft. On 8 April 1939 Douglas received an order for 144 aircraft.

XBT-2 with reconfigured tail, similar to BT-1 prototype.

Stratus coll.

SBD-1

During preparations for production, the design team introduced some more alterations. The engine cowling shape was improved, and it was fitted with a tear-drop profile carburettor fairing at the top. The propeller hub was covered with a spinner. The two 90 US gal. (341 l) main fuel tanks in the wing centre section were supplemented with two 15 US gal. (57 l) ones in the outer wing. Production aircraft were powered by the R-1820032 Cyclone engine rated at 1,000 hp for take-off and 950 hp nominal.

The aircraft could carry a 500, 1,000 or 1,600 lb bomb on a special carrier under the fuselage, and 100 lb bombs on under-wing carriers. It was armed with two 0.5 in Browning M-1 machine guns in the upper forward fuselage and with a single flexible 0.303 in Browning in the radio-operator/gunner's position.

Despite a larger original contract, only 57 aircraft were built of this variant, as it was assumed that an aircraft without armoured crew positions and with no self-sealing tanks was not fit for service. The very short range of the original Dauntless was another factor. The aircraft built were handed over to USMC units, and were not going to be used from aircraft-carriers.

SBD-1s had BuNos. 1596-1631 and 1735-1755.

Some aircraft of this version were fitted with cameras for reconnaissance missions. Such aircraft were designated SBD-1P.

SBD-1. 1/72 scale.

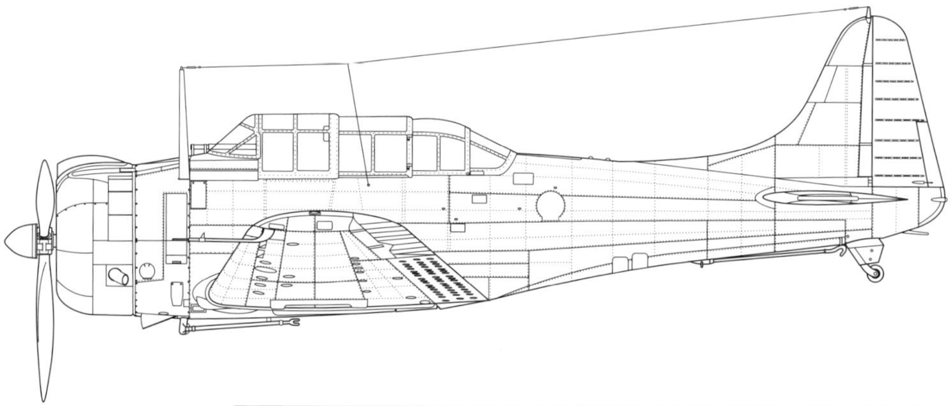

Right:
SBD-1 just before delivery to Marine Corps Bombing Squadron 1, summer 1940.
McDonnell Douglas.

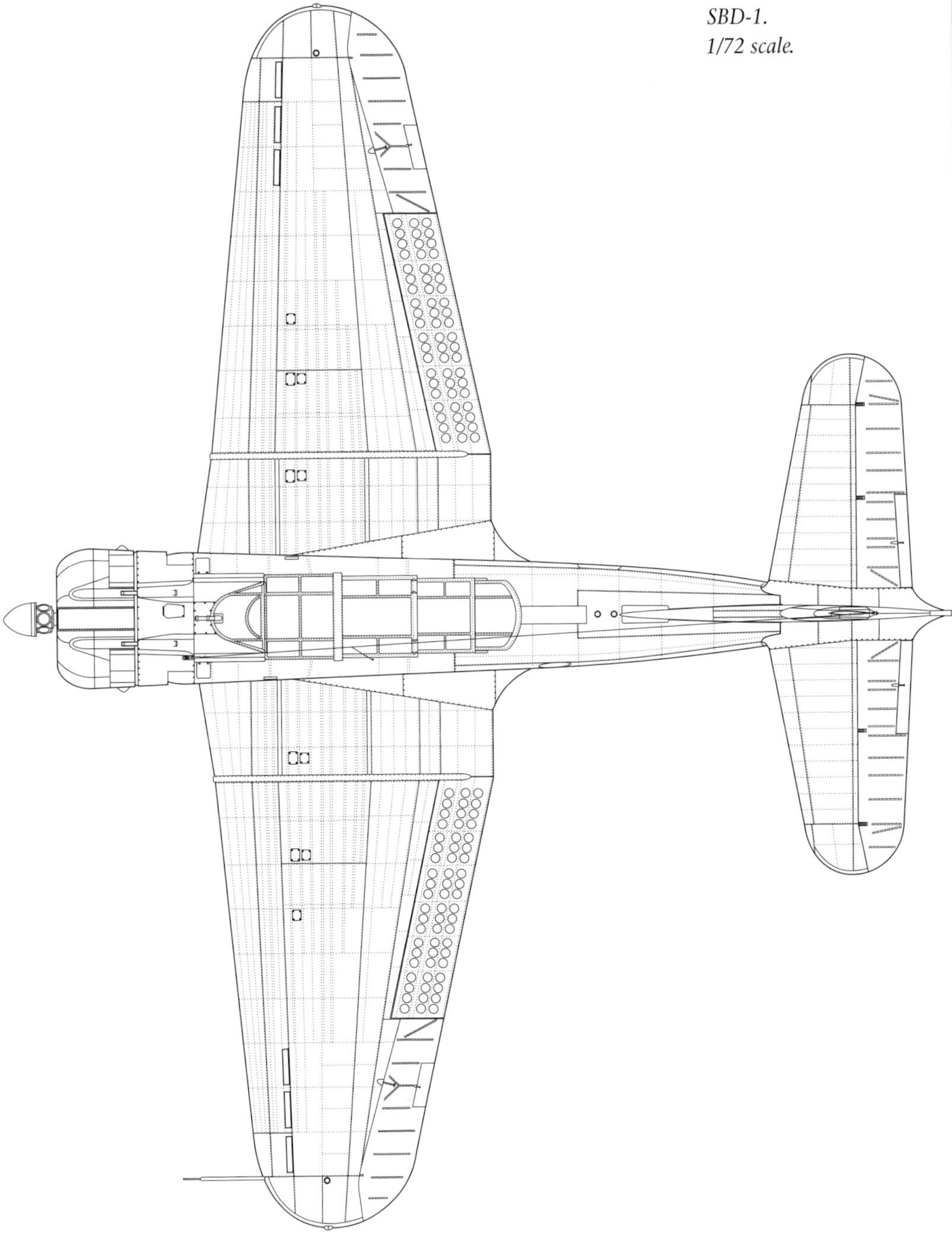

SBD-1.
1/72 scale.

SBD-2

The main alteration compared to the previous version was an increase in the fuel capacity. Instead of two 15 US gallon tanks, two 65 US gallon ones were fitted in the outer wing panels. No fire protection of the fuel system or crew armour was introduced, however. To retain the centre of gravity (CoG) position, one of the forward-firing machine guns was removed. The carburettor air intake was also reduced in size, and a Sperry automatic pilot was introduced.

This version covered the remaining 87 aircraft from the original US Navy orders, BuNos. 2102-2188.

The SBD-2 was the first Dauntless version to operate from aircraft-carriers.

Fourteen were converted for photo reconnaissance and designated SBD-2P.

SBD-2. 1/72 scale.

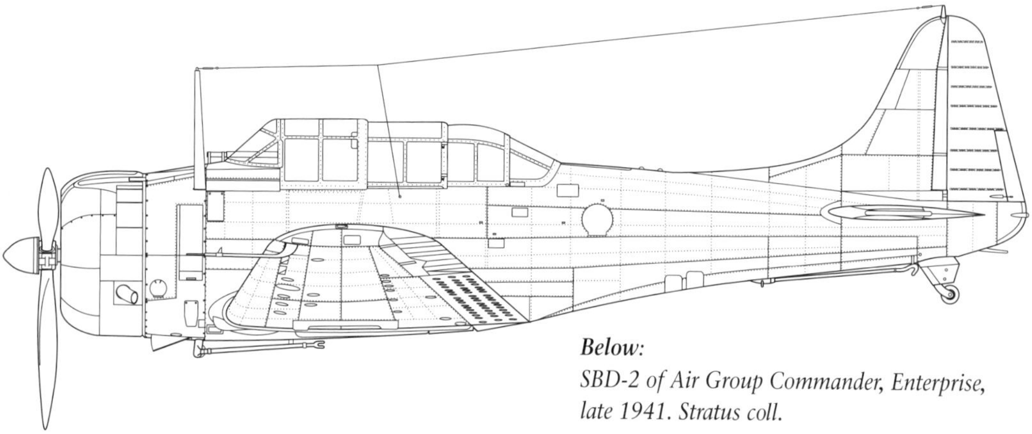

Below: SBD-2 of Air Group Commander, Enterprise, late 1941. Stratus coll.

SBD-3

This version introduced self-sealing tanks, which led to a reduction in the total fuel capacity. Two 75 US gallon tanks were fitted in the wing centre section, and two 55 US gallon ones in the outer wing panels. Cockpit armour weighing 176 lb was introduced, plus an armoured glass windscreen.

A Wright Cyclone R-1820-52 engine was fitted under a modified cowling with enlarged cooling flaps. Most SBD-3 had the spinners removed in service.

The first 174 aircraft of the version were ordered by the French Aeronavale, but after France surrendered in 1940 these were taken over by the US Navy.

A second forward-firing gun was re-introduced during production, and the single radio-operator/gunner's machine gun was replaced with twin guns of the same type. The introduction of twin guns necessitated redesign of the way the guns retracted into the fuselage. From mid-1942 the twin guns were retro-fitted to earlier production SBD-3s.

A total of 585 aircraft of this version was built, BuNos. 4518-4691 (the batch originally intended for the Aeronavale), 03185-03384 and 06492-06701.

43 aircraft were converted for photo reconnaissance duties and designated SBD-3P.

SBD-3, BuNo 4518, at Douglas factory, March 1941.

Stratus coll.

SBD-3.
1/72 scale.

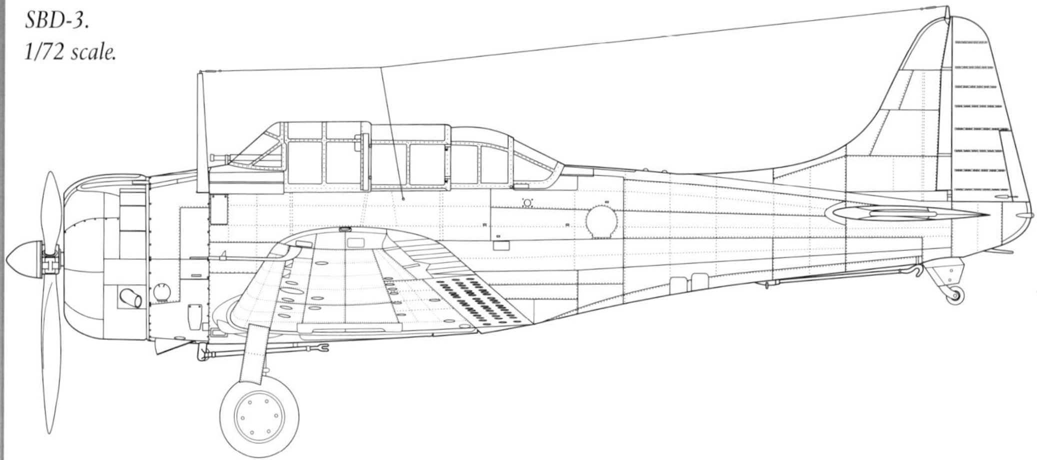

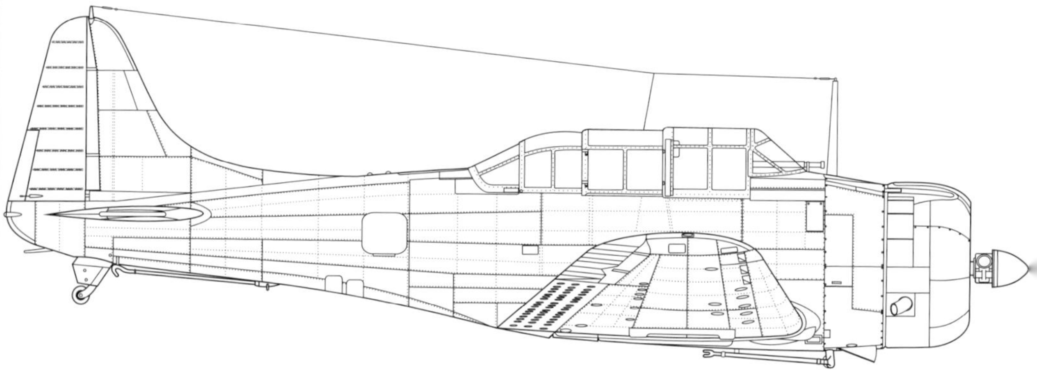

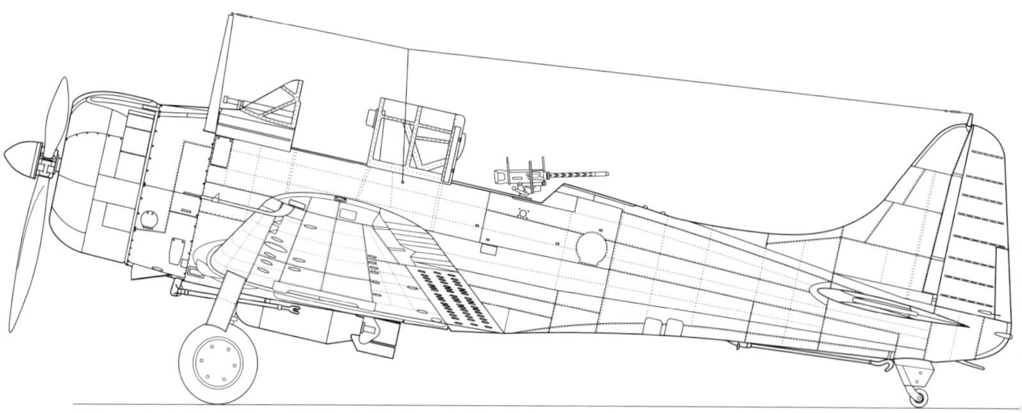

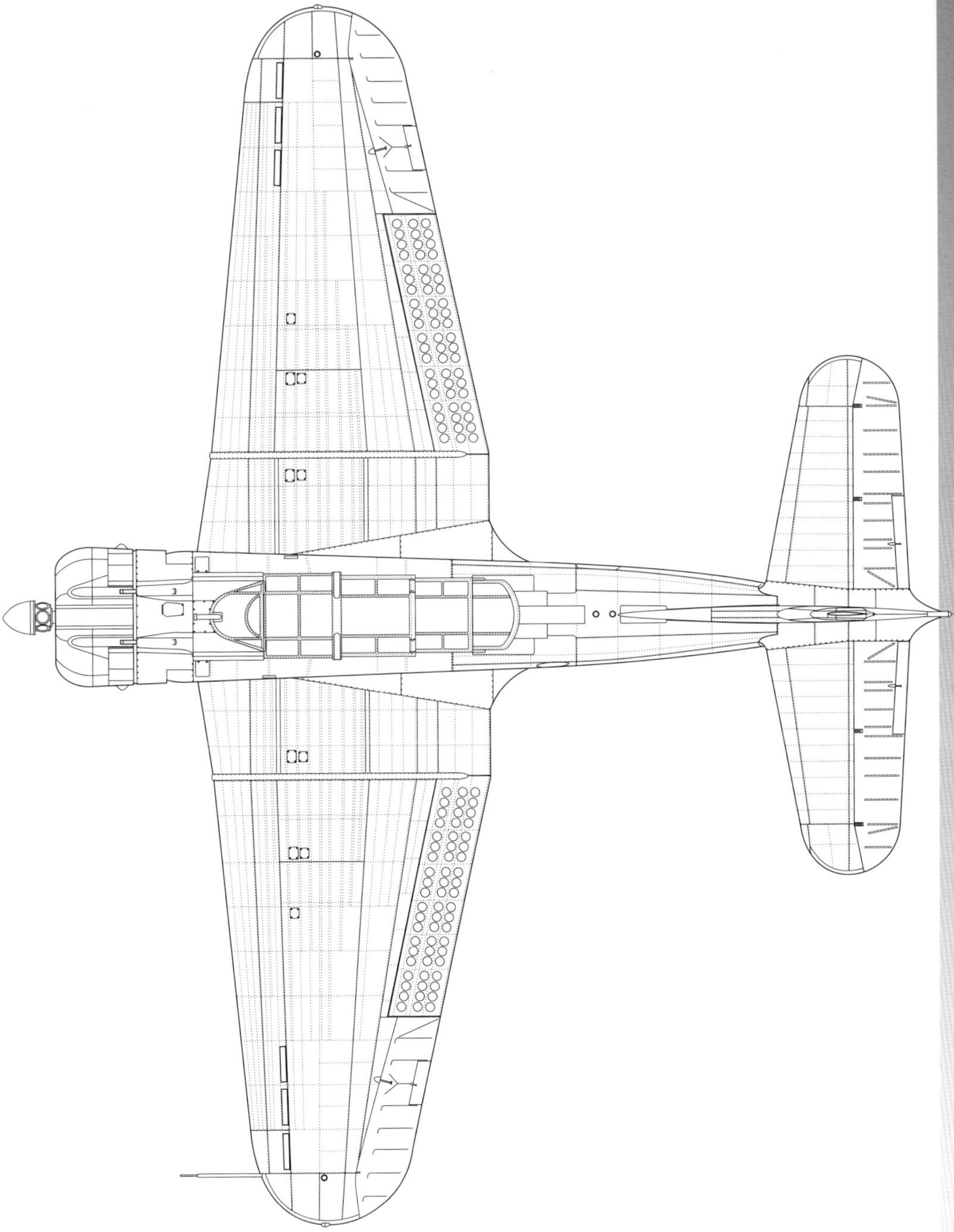

SBD-3.
1/72 scale.

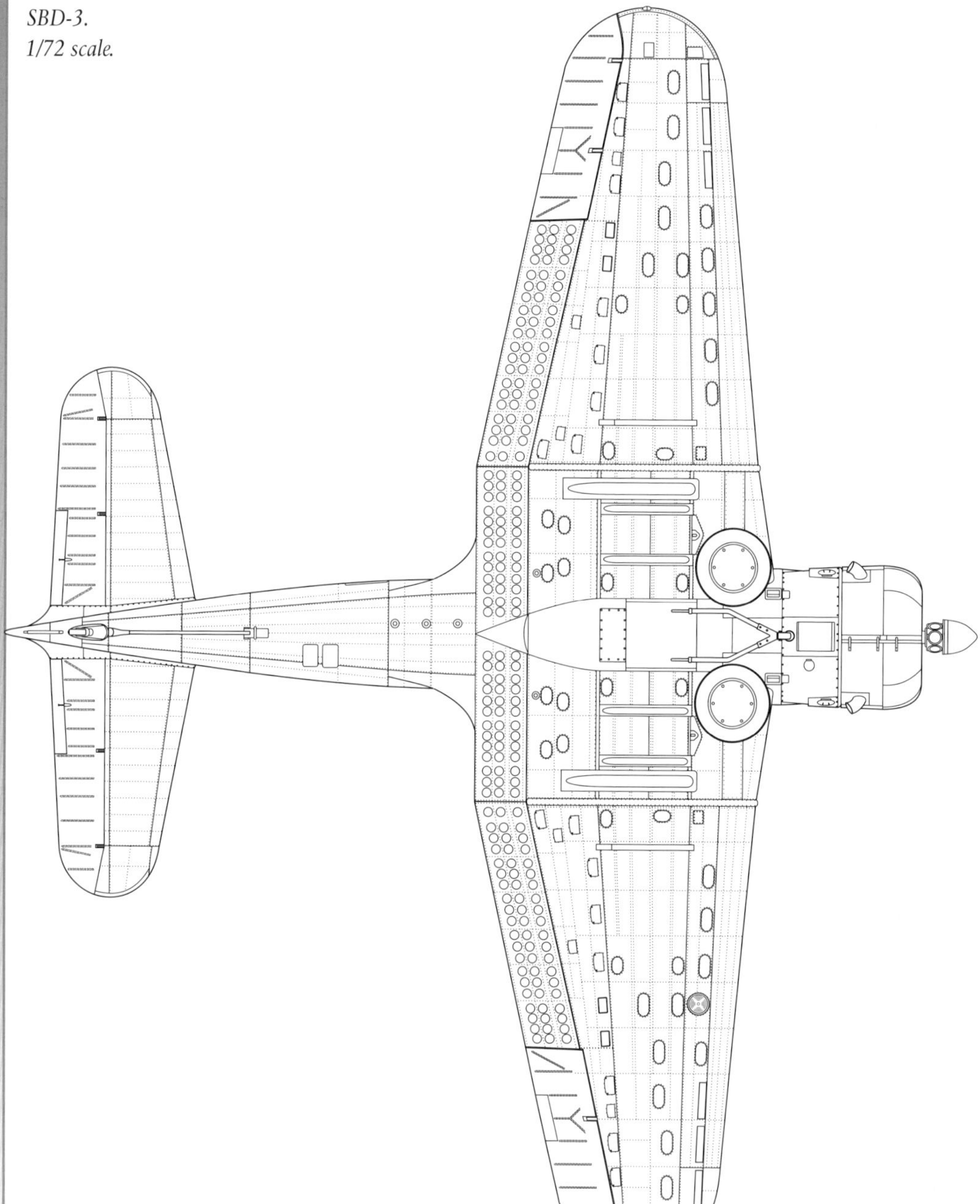

SBD-3.
1/72 scale.

SBD-3. Front view.
1/72 scale.

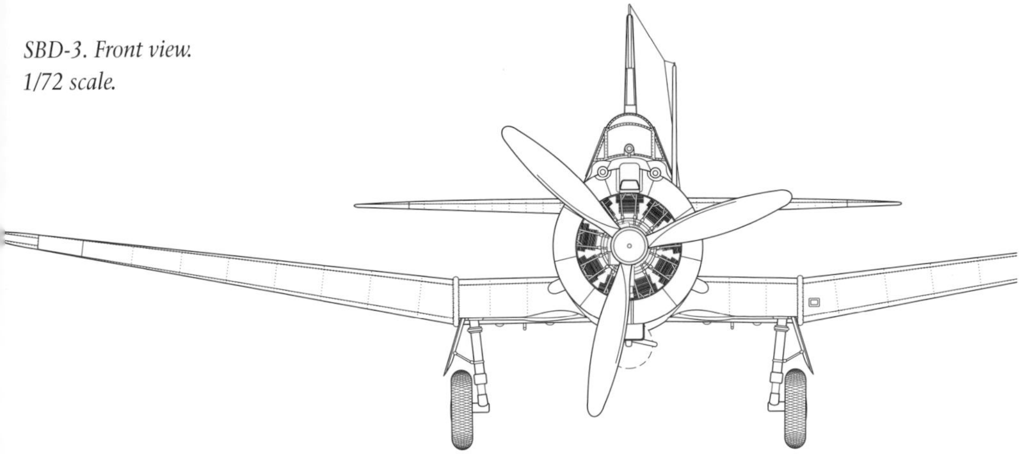

Left:
SBD-3, 41-S-9 of VS-41 on USS Ranger, during Operation Torch, November, 1942.
via Air Group 4 website.

Left:
SBD-3 of Bombing 3 on Enterprise, during the attack on Wake Island, February 1943.
USN.

SBD-4

The principal modification introduced in this version was the change of the electrical system from 12 V to 24 V. This allowed the aircraft to take a broader range of avionics, radio-navigation aids and radar. However, due to lack of equipment ready for use the aircraft were not factory-fitted with these. It would be during operations that most Dauntlesses of this version were equipped with radar at modification centres. Yagi aerials were fitted under each wing.

Another important modification was to introduce a new propeller, the Hamilton Standard Hydromatic constant speed unit. At the same time the use of a spinner was discontinued.

The fuel system was improved by introduction of two electric pumps, main and back-up ones.

Many SBD-4s went to units operating from land bases, these aircraft were fitted with larger tail wheels with tyres, and were not fitted with arrestor hooks.

A total of 870 SBD-4 Dauntlesses were built, and the aircraft were given numbers in the ranges of BuNos 06702-06991 and 10317-10806. Production continued from October 1942 to April 1943.

SBD-4 with 1,000lb G.P. bomb in place on the swinging crutch. Note also a Yagi radar antenna.
McDonnell Douglas.

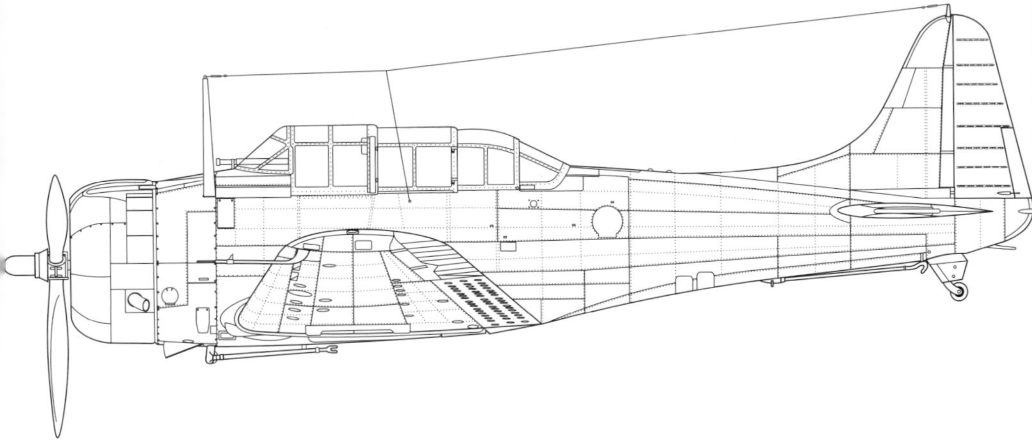

Above:
SBD-5. 1/72 scale.

SBD-5

This was the Dauntless version built in the greatest numbers. The aircraft was fitted with a more powerful engine, the Wright R-1820-60 Cyclone with a military rating of 1,200 hp.

The new engine required substantial redesign of the cowling. The number of cooling flaps was reduced from three to one on each side, and the louvre was enlarged and repositioned to the rear. The carburettor air intake was moved from the top of the cowling.

The aircraft was modified to carry two 58 US gallon external fuel tanks. It was fitted with the modern Mk VIII reflector sight, which replaced the previous telescopic sight. The ring sight for the fixed machine guns was replaced by the Mk IX sight. The aircraft was fitted with heated windscreen, to prevent the glazing from misting over in a dive.

Below:
SBD-5. Note that this aircraft does not have the radar antenna.
A. Lochte coll.

Between February 1943 and April 1944 a total of 2,965 were built, in the ranges of BuNos. 10807-10956, 10957-11066, 28059-28829, 28831-29213, 35922-36421, 36433-36932, and 54050-54599.

SBD-5.
1/72 scale.

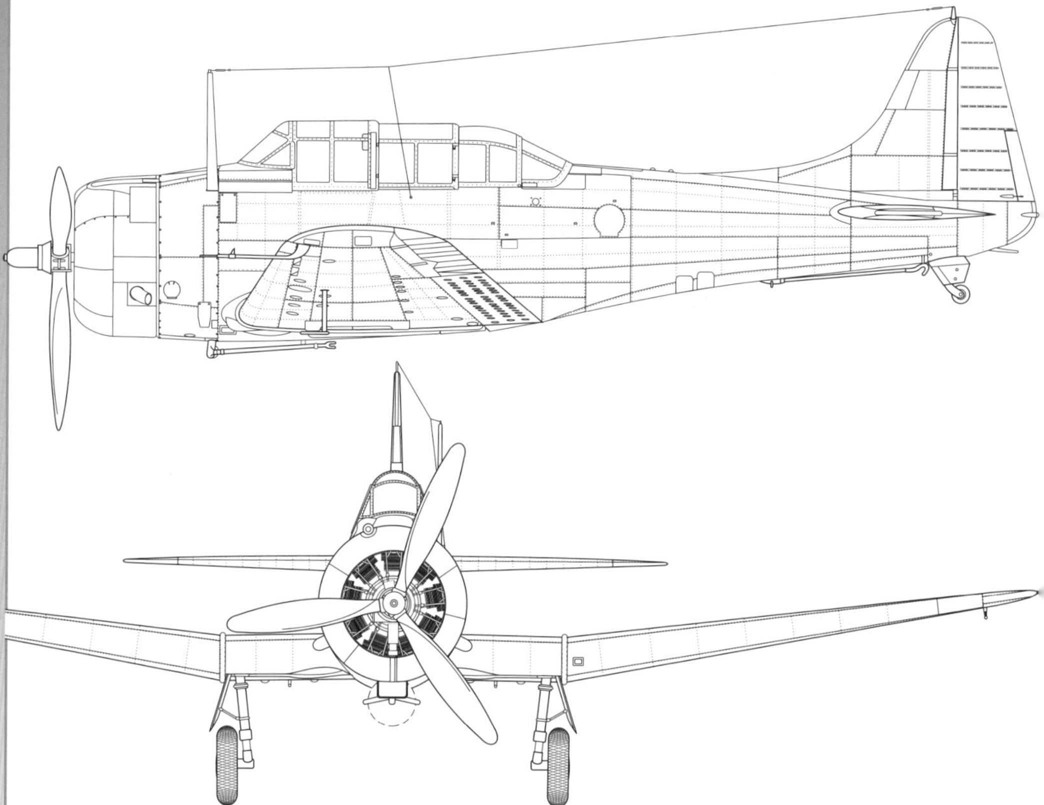

Right:
SBD-5 of VB-10 on patrol over Enterprise, during the Palau raids, 29-30 March 1944

A. Lochte coll.

SBD-5 taking off.
A. Lochte coll.

SBD-5.
A. Lochte coll.

SBD-5
Stratus coll.

SBD-6

This was the last Dauntless version. It was powered by an even more powerful R-1820-66 engine rated at 1,350 hp. Metal fuel tanks were replaced with plastic ones, with a total capacity of 284 US gallons. Aircraft of the version were factory fitted with radar.

A total of 450 aircraft were built, in the range of BuNos. 54600-55049. The last Dauntless, no. 55049, left the assembly line on 22 July 1944.

SBD-6 of VMSB-231, Marine Corps, over Task Force 58. Amjuro anchorage, early 1944.
A. Lochte coll.

A-24 Banshee

In July 1940 the USAAC borrowed several SBD-1s from US Marine Corps units for testing. The aircraft were tested operationally by the 24th Bomb Squadron USAAC for their usefulness in army service.

On 27 September 1940 the US War Department placed an order for 78 aircraft designated A-24-DE from Douglas Aircraft. The aircraft received serial nos. 41-15746 to 41-15823.

The A-24 was nearly identical with the naval SBD-3. No arrestor hook was fitted, but its mount was retained. A pneumatic tyre (rather than solid-rubber) tail wheel was fitted. Army-type radio equipment was used. A-24s did not have flare launchers in the rear fuselage, so their covers were not fitted, either.

Additionally 90 SBD-3s were delivered to the USAAF and these were designated the SBD-3A. Compared to the naval variant they had similar changes to those introduced in the A-24.

A-24A-DE

These aircraft were identical to the SBD-4 and were modified for land-based operations, similar to the A-24.

They were given serial numbers in the ranges 42-6772 to 42- 6831 and 42-60772 to 42-60881.

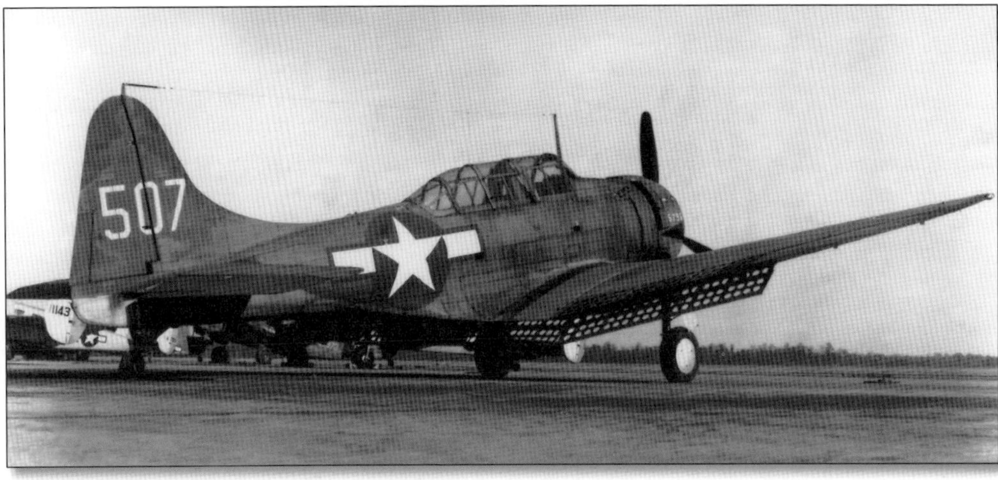

A-24A, serial 42-60794 at Selma Field.
A. Lochte coll.

A-24B

The aircraft were identical to the SBD-5, except for the changes listed above. They were built both by the Douglas El Segundo plant, designated the A-24B-DE, and at Tulsa, Oklahoma, designated the A-24B-DT.

The Tulsa plant built 615 A-24B-DTs, with the following serial numbers:

A-24B-DT-1 – 42-54285 to 42-54399
A-24B-DT-5 – 42-54400 to 42-54459
A-24B-DT-10 – 42-54460 to 42-54649
A-24B-DT-15 – 42-54650 to 42-54899

Additionally, 60 A-24Bs (42-60882 to 42-60941) eventually went to the US Marine Corps as the SBD-5A, serialled BuNos. 09693 to 09752.

F-24B

A number of A-24s remained in service after 1948 and were re-designated the F-24B.

Special versions:

Douglas QF-24A-DE Dauntless c/n 1538, originally A-24A-DE 42-6783 remanufactured as drone aircraft, redesignated RA-24A in 1948.

Douglas RA-24A. Conversion to a radio operated drone with receiving equipment.

A-24A.
1/72 scale.

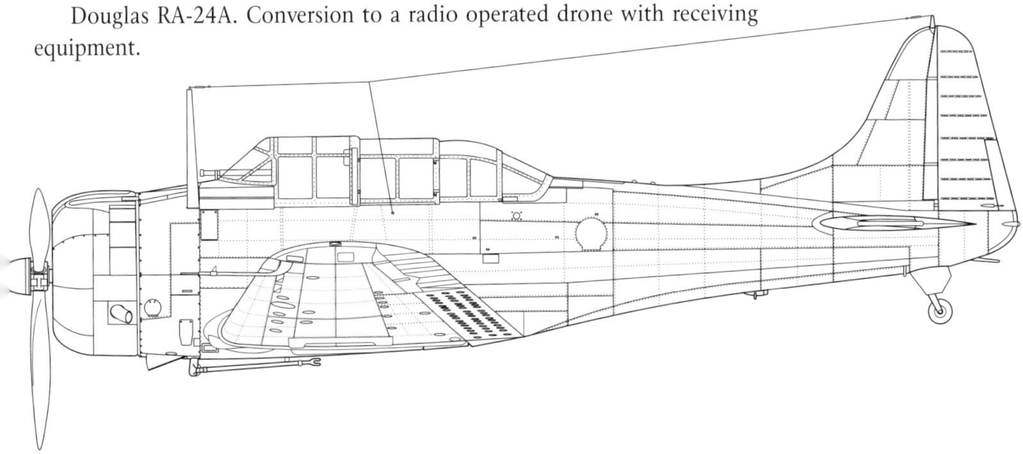

This page:
Douglas A-24 S/N 41-15746, the first A-24.
U.S. Air Force.

Above: *A-24B formation. Nearest aircraft is A-24B-1-DT, S/N 42-54298 "Bar Fly;" third aircraft is "Marye D.". U.S. Air Force.*
Below: *Douglas RA-24B-15-DT (S/N 42-54736) on Morotai on Jan. 1, 1945. RA - indicated a Restricted category — not suitable for combat. U.S. Air Force*

DOUGLAS SBD DAUNTLESS/A-24 BANSHEE SPECIFICATION

Variant	BT-1	SBD-1	SBD-2	SBD-3	SBD-4	SBD-5	SBD-6	A-24-DE SBD-3A	A-24A-DE SBD-4A	A-24B-DE SBD-5A
Dimensions and weights:										
Wing span [ft]	41’ 6 3/8”	41’ 6 3/8”	41’ 6 3/8”	41’ 6 3/8”	41’ 6 3/8”	41’ 6 3/8”	41’ 6 3/8”	41’ 6 3/8”	41’ 6 3/8”	41’ 6 3/8”
[m]	12.65	12.65	12.65	12.65	12.65	12.65	12.65	12.65	12.65	12.65
Length [ft]	31’ 8”	32’ 1”	32’ 1”	32’ 8	32’ 8”	33’	33’	32’ 8	32’ 8	33’
[m]	9.65	9.78	9.78	9.96	9.96	10.06	10.06	9.96	9.96	10,06
Height [ft]	12’ 6”	13’ 7”	13’ 7”	13’ 7”	13’ 7”	13’ 7”	13’ 7”	13’ 7”	13’ 7”	13’ 7”
[m]	3.81	4.14	4.14	4.14	4.14	4.14	4.14	4.14	4.14	4.14
Wing area [sq ft]	319.0	325.0	325.0	325.0	325.0	325.0	325.0	325.0	325.0	325.0
[m²]	29.64	30.19	30.19	30.19	30.19	30.19	30.19	30.19	30.19	30.19
Empty weight [lb]	4,605	5,903	6,293	6,345	6,360	6,533	6,554	6,265	6,360	6,330
[kg]	2 089	2 678	2 855	2 878	2 885	2 963	2 973	2 842	2 885	2 871
Max. take-off weight [lb]	7,060	9,790	10,360	10,400	10,480	10,700	10,882	10,200	10,480	10,450
[kg]	3 202	4 441	4 699	4 717	4 754	4 854	4 936	4 627	4 754	4 740
Powerplant:										
Engine variant	P & W R-1535-94	Wright R-1820-32	Wright R-1820-32	Wright R-1820-52	Wright R-1820-52	Wright R-1820-60	Wright R-1820-66	Wright R-1820-52	Wright R-1820-52	Wright R-1820-60
Rated at [hp]	825	1 000	1 000	1 000	1 000	1 200	1 350	1 000	1 000	1 200
[kW]	615	746	746	746	746	895	1007	746	746	895
Performance:										
Maximum speed [mph]	222	253	252	250	245	252	262	250	246	253
[km/h]	357	407	405	402	394	405	421	402	396	407
Cruising speed [mph]	192	142	148	152	150	139	143	173	150	180
[km/h]	309	228	238	244	241	224	230	279	241	290
Climb rate [ft/min]	1,270	1,730	1,080	1,190	1,150	1,700	1,710	-	-	-
[m/min]	387	527	329	363	351	518	521	-	-	-
Operational ceiling [ft]	25,300	29,600	26,000	27,100	26,700	24,300	28,600	26,100	27,000	-
[m]	7 710	9 020	7 920	8 260	8 140	7 410	8 720	7 960	8 230	-
Scouting mission range [miles]	-	860	1,225	1,345	1,300	1,115	1,230	950	975	950
[km]	-	1 380	1 970	2 160	2 090	1 790	1 980	1 530	1 570	1 530
Bombing mission range [miles]	1,150	1,165	1,370	1,580	1,450	1,565	1,700	1,300	1,300	1,250
[km]	1 850	1 870	2 200	2 540	2 330	2 520	2 740	2 090	2 090	2 010

Technical Description

The Douglas SBD Dauntless was a two-seat, single-engine dive bomber and reconnaissance aircraft, an all-metal low-wing monoplane.

The design of the Dauntless drew heavily on experience with the Northrop Alpha and Gamma all-metal monoplanes, and had a very strong structure (it was certified to loads from +9g to –4g). The SBD-1 and SBD-2 airframe structure was made of duralumin, from the SBD-3 it used Alclad 24ST (aluminium alloy sheets with rolled-on layer of pure aluminium to protect from corrosion).

The cantilever wings had a NACA 2415-2409 airfoil. The wing structure was multi-bay, typical for all Northrop all-metal low-wing monoplanes. The wing centre section was nearly rectangular in planform. Tapered outer wing panels were attached to it. Detachable wing tips were nearly semi-circular. Unusually for a carrier-borne aircraft, the wings of the Dauntless could not be folded for stowage.

Fixed slats were fitted on the leading edges of the wings (known as the 'letter box', as they resembled the slot in the letter box), three on each wing. The ailerons had metal structure with fabric covering. The port aileron was fitted with a metal trim tab. Five-section spoiler-flaps were fitted, hydraulically actuated by a single jack. The three lower flap segments, two on the wings and one under the wing centre section, deflected downwards to a maximum angle of 42° for take-off and landing. In a dive, the upper segments were also deflected (up to 37.5°) in addition to the lower segments. Flaps were perforated with 1.74 in (4.45 cm) holes over their entire surface.

A retractable landing light was fitted under the port wing. Check lights for the carrier landing approach control system were fitted in the leading edge.

Catapult attachments were fitted on the wing undersurface immediately aft of the main wheel wells.

A-24B-15-DT.

A. Lochte coll.

The semi-monococque fuselage structure consisted of channel profile frames, to which pressed longerons and smooth duralumin skin sheets were attached. The wing centre section was integral with the lower forward fuselage. The rear fuselage, aft of the cockpit, was split by solid frames into watertight compartments to provide proper buoyancy when ditching. The SBD-1 and SBD-2 carried two inflatable floats on sides of the fuselage forward of the cockpit. These were abandoned from the SBD-3 onwards.

The tail surfaces were conventional, with the fin and tailplane covered with duralumin sheets. The fin was integral with the fuselage. Rudder and elevators had metal structure, fabric covered, and were fitted with trim tabs.

It had a tail wheel layout retractable undercarriage. Carrier-borne versions (SBD) used a solid rubber tail wheel, land-based versions and the A-24 had pneumatic tyres. The attachment for ground towing of the aircraft was fitted aft of the tail wheel. The arrestor hook was fitted under the rear fuselage.

The aircraft was powered by the Wright R-1820 Cyclone 9-cylinder radial. The engine was attached on a steel tube mount, and housed in a NACA cowling. The engine drove a three-blade variable pitch, feathering Hamilton Standard propeller. From the SBD-4 constant-speed Hamilton Standard Hydromatic propellers were fitted. The propeller diameter was 10 ft 10 in (3.3 m).

Fuel tanks were located in the wing centre section and in the outer wing panels.

An oil cooler was fitted in the lower engine cowling with an adjustable air intake.

Cockpit equipment. The pilot's cockpit was located forward, with the radio-operator/gunner's compartment behind. The windscreen was made of bullet-proof glass (starting from the SBD-3). The pilot's cockpit hood slid back to open, that of the radio-operator/gunner slid forward. A window in the bottom of the cockpit allowed the pilot to see below the aircraft. Hoisting cable attachments were located on the sides of the cockpit (the cable was permanently attached to them, and was stored in the cockpit at all times), these allowed the aircraft to be slung under the roof of the hangar deck on an aircraft-carrier. The overturn pylon was located aft of the pilot's seat. Cockpit equipment included a full radio set, and a Sperry automatic pilot.

The rear compartment included a back-up set of controls, to allow control by the other crew member in emergency. Signal flare discharger with ammunition magazine was located in the rear compartment.

The cockpit was fitted with an oxygen system for both crew members.

Life raft with food and water emergency rations was located aft of the cockpit, in a cylinder with a separate cover on the port side of the fuselage.

Baggage compartment hatch was located on the starboard side of the fuselage.

US Navy unit operation principles

US Navy air combat units were split into the following categories:
Fighting Squadrons (VF)
Torpedo Squadrons (VT)
Scouting Squadrons (VS)
Bombing Squadrons (VB)

Dauntlesses were used in Scouting and Bombing units.

Scouting Squadrons were further differentiated according to where they were based:

Scouting Squadrons (VS) based on aircraft-carriers and using single-engine, two-seat monoplanes, such as the SB2U, SBD and later the Curtis SB2C Helldiver.

Observation-Scouting (VOS) units, which used observation aircraft based on battleships and cruisers.

Land-based units, used mainly for anti-submarine duties. These units used mainly carrier-borne aircraft types, such as the SBD, or the OS2U with wheeled undercarriage.

Crews of carrier-based aircraft were trained for both Scout and typical bombing missions. Often the aircraft from VB units flew typical Scout missions. The crews were obliged to submit information about the enemy before commencing a bombing attack.

Typical Scout operations from aircraft-carriers involved missions of SBDs in nine pairs, each pair searching in a pie-shaped wedge sector 200 miles long and 20-50 miles wide (10^0).

SBD-3 on Ranger being refuelled, during Operation Torch, November, 1942.
via Air Group 4 website.

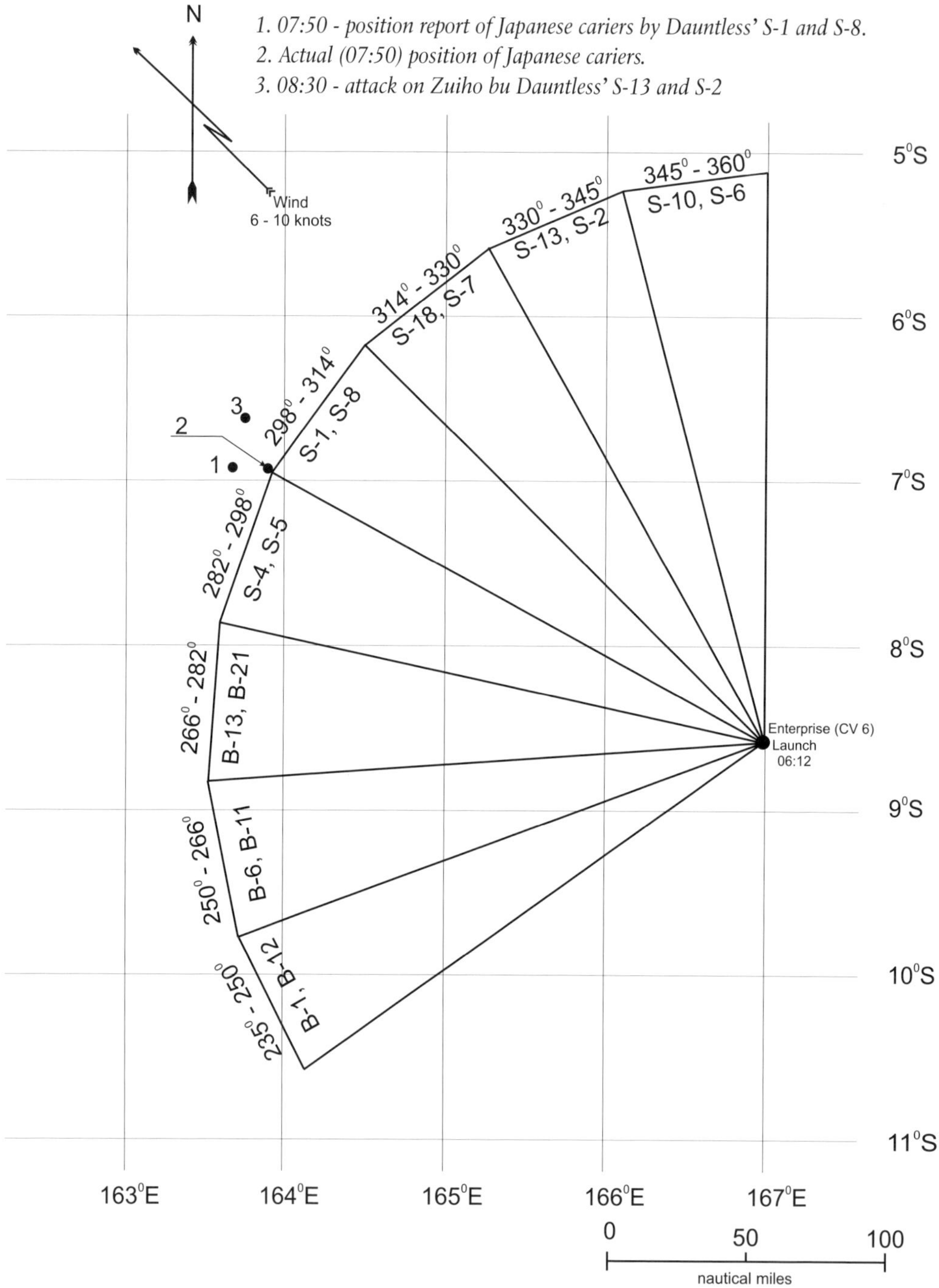

Typical Dauntless search pattern, flown by VB-10 and VS-10, Enterprise, 26 October 1942, battle of Santa Cruz.

Communication was essential during such missions and this was ensured by the radio-operator/gunner. Early in the war, during 1941-42, reports about detection of the enemy force and of its position were usually transmitted using Morse code, as being more reliable over longer ranges than voice/radio communication.

For a Scout mission the Dauntless carried a single 500 lb bomb, to give the aircraft longer range.

Bombing Squadrons (VB)

Dive bombing was the main role of the Dauntless. Full bombing attack was normally carried out by the whole squadron: 18 aircraft. The squadron was organised into three 6 aircraft divisions, each division consisting of two 3-aircraft sections.

A fully armed Dauntless on a bombing mission carried a single 1,000 lb general purpose (GP) or armour-piercing (AP) bomb (depending on the target type) under the fuselage and two 100 lb bombs under the wings. Fuse type also depended on the target type. Heavily armoured warships were attacked with delayed action bombs, so that the explosion took place deep inside the hull.

Typical path of a dive of 70° with pull-out acceleration about 4G.
Based on research by Peter C. Smith.

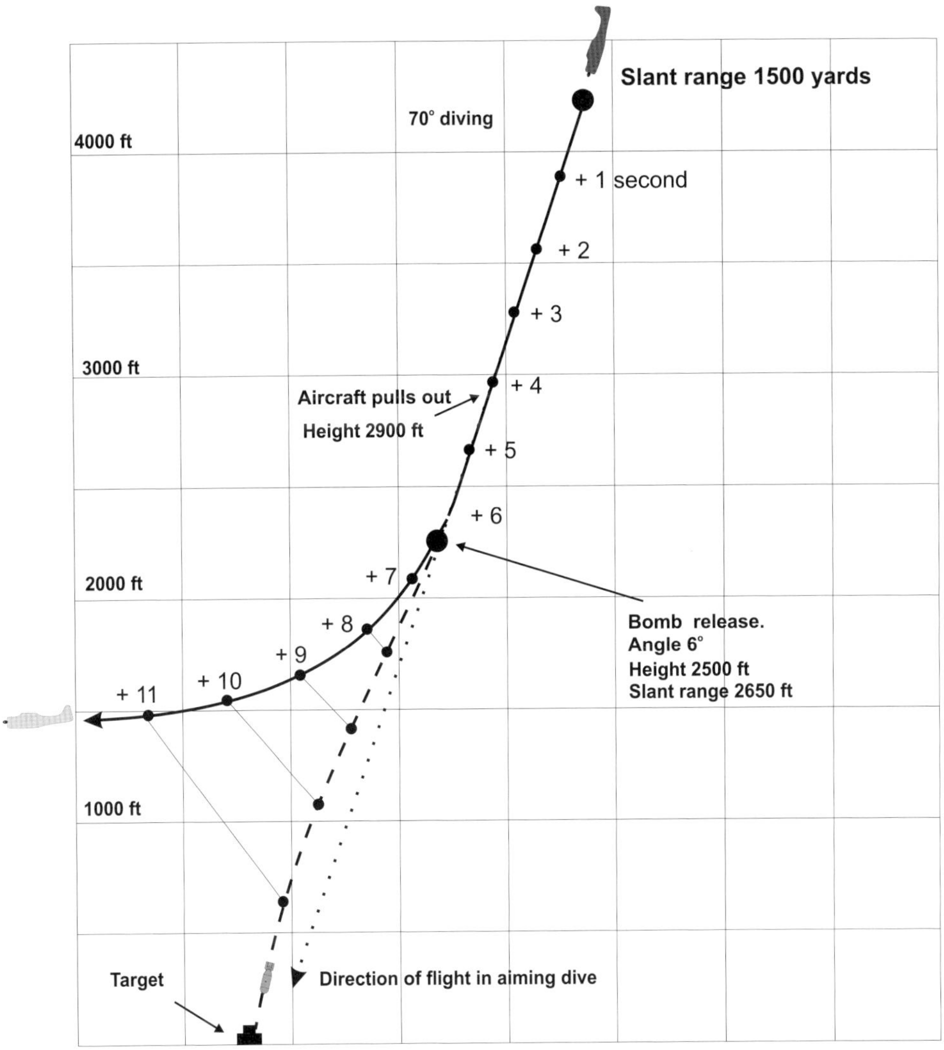

SBD US Navy Units

December 1941

Unit	Location	Aircraft
VB-2	USS Lexington (CV 2)	16 SBD-2
VS-2	USS Lexington (CV 2)	18 SBD-2/3
VB-3	USS Saratoga (CV 3)	21 SBD-3
VS-3	USS Saratoga (CV 3)	22 SBD-3
VB-5	USS Yorktown (CV 5)	19 SBD-3
VS-5	USS Yorktown (CV 5)	19 SBD-3
VB-6	USS Enterprise (CV 6)	18 SBD-2
VS-6	USS Enterprise (CV 6)	18 SBD-2/3
VMSB-132	Quantico, Virginia, USA	19 SBD-1
VMSB-232	Ewa, Hawaii, USA	22 SBD-1/2

June 1942 (outside continental USA)

Unit	Location	Aircraft
VB-3	USS Yorktown (CV 5)	18 SBD-3
VS-3	USS Saratoga (CV 3)	27 SBD-3
VB-5	USS Yorktown (CV 5)	19 SBD-3
VS-5	Hawaii	19 SBD-3
VB-6	USS Enterprise (CV 6)	19 SBD-3
VB-8	USS Hornet (CV 8)	19 SBD-3
VS-8	USS Hornet (CV 8)	19 SBD-3
VMSB-231	Hawaii	6 SBD-1
VMSB-232	Hawaii	Unknown
VMSB-233	Hawaii	Unknown
VMSB-234	Hawaii	5 SBD-1
VMSB-241	Midway	19 SBD-2

Operation Torch – November 1942

Unit	Location	Aircraft
VS-41	USS Ranger (CV 4)	18 SBD-3
VGS-26	USS Sangamon (ACV 26)	9 SBD-3
VGS-29	USS Santee (ACV 29)	9 SBD-3

SBD-3 during Operation Torch, November, 1942.
via Air Group 4 website.

June 1943 (outside continental USA)

Unit	Location	Aircraft
VB-3	USS Saratoga (CV 3)	18 SBD-3/4
VB-9	USS Essex (CV 9)	16 SBD-4
VB-11	Guadalcanal	18 SBD-3
VB-12	Hawaii	19 SBD-3
VB-13	USS Saratoga (CV 3)	17 SBD-3/4
VB-21	Guadalcanal	19 SBD-3
VB-22	Hawaii	19 SBD-3/4
VS-23	USS Princeton (CVL 23)	9 SBD-4
VC-26	Efate, New Hebrides	9 SBD-3
VC-28	Efate, New Hebrides	9 SBD-3
VMSB-132	Espiritu Santo	45 SBD-3
VMSB-141	Auckland, New Zealand	21 SBD-2/3/4
VMSB-142	Nandi and Efate	37 SBD-3/4
VMSB-144	Guadalcanal	21 SBD (diff. ver.)
VMSB-151	Fanafuti and Samoa	20 SBD (diff. ver.)
VMSB-234	Nandi	15 SBD-4
VMSB-235	Midway	17 SBD (diff. ver.)
VMSB-235	Hawaii	18 SBD (diff. ver.)
VMSB-241	Tutuila, Samoa	21 SBD-4
VMSB-243	Johnston Island	15 SBD (diff. ver.)
VMSB-244	Midway	23 SBD (diff. ver.)

1944 (outside continental USA)

Unit	Location	June 1944	December 1944
VB-10	USS Enterprise (CV 6)	21 SBD-5	
VB-16	USS Lexington (CV 16)	34 SBD-5	
VB-100	Barbers Point, Hawaii (RAG)	9 SBD-5	7 SBD-5
VB-305	Segi Field	24 SBD-5	
VB-306	Torokina, Bougainville	22 SBD-5	
VS-46	Pearl Harbour	12 SBD-5	12 SBD-5
VS-47	Johnston and Palymra Islands	18 SBD-4	17 SBD-4
VS-52	Roi, Marshalls	12 SBD-5	13 SBD-5
VS-53	Pearl Harbour	18 SBD-5	18 SBD-5
VS-51	Tutuila, Samoa	14 SBD-5	
VS-54	Guadalcanal	16 SBD-3/4	
VS-55	Espiritu Santo	10 SBD-4	
VS-57	Noumea, New Caledonia	23 SBD-4	
VS-58	Efate, New Hebrides	10 SBD-4	
VS-64	Espiritu Santo	10 SBD-5	
VS-65	Fanafuti	15 SBD-4	
VS-66	Tarawa Atoll	14 SBD-5	15 SBD-5
VS-67	Nandi	10 SBD-3/4	
VS-68	Treasury Islands	10 SBD-4	
VS-69	Pearl Harbour	18 SBD-5	18 SBD-6
VMSB-133	Ewa, Hawaii / Torokina	20 SBD-5	23 SBD-6
VSMB-142	Ewa, Hawaii / Emirau	34 SBD-5	20 SBD-6
VMSB-151	Engebi, Eniwetok Atoll	26 SBD-5	24 SBD-5
VMSB-231	Majuro Atoll	22 SBD-5	
VMSB-235	Efate, New Hebrides	19 SBD-4/5	
VMSB-236	Torokina, Bougainville	22 SBD-5	23 SBD-6
VMSB-241	Emirau /Munda	21 SBD-5	22 SBD-6
VSMB-243	Emirau		25 SBD-6
VMSB-244	Emirau / Green Island	18 SBD-5	25 SBD-5
VMSB-245	Makin Island / Majuro Atoll	20 SBD-5	24 SBD-6
VMSB-331	Majuro Atoll	22 SBD-5	
VMSB-332	Midway	26 SBD-4/5	
VSMB-341	Green Island		21 SBD-6
VSMB-343	Midway		10 SBD-5

July 1945 (outside continental USA)

Unit	Location	Aircraft
VMSB-133	Cotobato, PI	24 SBD-6
VMSB -142	Zamboanga, PI	24 SBD-6
VMSB -236	Zamboanga, PI	24 SBD-6
VMSB -241	Cotobato, PI	24 SBD-6
VMSB -243	Zamboanga, PI	24 SBD-6
VSMB-341	Zamboanga, PI	24 SBD-6

A-24 Banshee Units

The Army A-24 version of the Douglas dive bomber never achieved the degree of success as did its Navy SBD counterpart.

The first A-24 was delivered to the Army on June 17, 1941. The first operational A-24 unit was the new 27th Bombardment Group (L) based at Savannah, Georgia, USA. Three of the four squadrons of the 27th BG were equipped with the A-24, plus one squadron of the 3rd Bombardment Group. The remaining squadrons of these groups were equipped with A-20A

The 27th BG was in the process of been shipped to the Philippines when the war in the Pacific broke out. The crews were in the Philippines, but their aircraft were on their way via ship from Honolulu. The shipment was diverted to Australia, where they arrived on December 22. Some of the 27th BG pilots were evacuated from the Philippines to join their aircraft in Australia. Eleven A-24s flew up to Java in February of 1942, but this battle was already lost. The remainder began operations from Port Moresby with the 8th Bombardment Squadron on April 1, 1942. These units suffered heavy losses in the face of the Japanese advance.

The A-24 was never very popular with its crews, and most of them were retained in the USA for training duties. Following the New Guinea debacle, only one other squadron was to take the A-24 into combat. This was the 58th Bombardment Squadron (Dive), based at Wheeler Field in Hawaii. After carrying out an attack on Kiska Island in the Aleutians on August 4, 1943, the 58th BG was transferred to the Gilbert Islands and redesignated the 531st Fighter-Bomber Squadron. In December of 1943, The 531st fighter Bomber Squadron operated their A-24Bs briefly but successfully from bases in the Makin Islands.

After the war, several A-24s still remained in service with the USAAF. When the 'A-for-attack' designation was eliminated in 1948, the few surviving A-24s were redesignated F-24.

Foreign Users

UK - Royal Navy

In February 1944 nine obsolete SBD-5s were delivered to Britain for tests with the FAA, four of the aircraft were subsequently handed over to the RAF for their own tests.

Although they were never used operationally, they were given the official British designation of Dauntless DB Mk I.

BuNo.	Royal Navy serial	Fate
36022	JS997	
36023	JS998	To RAF
36456	JS999	
54191	JS923	To RAF
54192	JS924	
54193	JS925	To RAF
54194	JS926	To RAF
54195	JS927	
54196	JS928	

SBD-5, Dauntless I, serial JS997 in RAF markings, tested at RAE Farnboough, 1944.

IWM.

SBD-4 still with US markings, at what is probably Whenuapai in August 1943. Note the well worn paint, and the roughly painted number on the fuselage.

Official RNZAF via M. Laird

New Zealand

The RNZAF used a total of 69 Dauntlesses (NZ5001–NZ5068, BuNo 28452) during 1943–1944. Initially the order called for 206 A-24 aircraft delivered in 1943 and 1944, but eventually none were delivered. Faced with the delay, the RNZAF borrowed 27 SBD-3 and SBD-4 aircraft from the Marine Air Group 14 (MAG-14). The aircraft were allocated to 25 (Dive Bomber) Squadron. The SBD-3s were initially operated with US markings and temporary RNZAF numbers. They were serialled NZ205 to NZ222, later changed to NZ5001–NZ5018. The SBD-4s were serialled NZ5019 to NZ5027. The Dauntlesses were formally handed over to New Zealand in November 1943. 25 Sqn pilots underwent extensive training in these aircraft.

RNZAF SBDs leaving Piva for a strike on Rabaul. Middle aircraft is NZ5062, the only surviving RNZAF SBD-5. Aircraft are fully armed with 2 x 250lb and 1 x 500lb bomb.

Official RNZAF via M. Laird

In March 1944 25 Sqn took delivery of SBD-5s (NZ5046-NZ5063), and the worn out SBD-3s and SBD-4s were handed over to other units as training aircraft, and served there until February 1944.

SBD-5s delivered to 25 Sqn were fitted with pneumatic tyre tail wheels and no arrestor hook. From March on the unit operated from Piva airfield in Bougainville. 25 Squadron operated in the area for the next 8 weeks, making 29 attacks (average of 95 flying hours per crew).

Squadron pilots flew a total of 530 combat missions in 1,750 hours, dropping 280 tonnes of bombs. Two aircraft were lost due to enemy fire and three more to other causes in combat missions. The squadron was disbanded in May 1944.

Right: *SBD-4 of 25 (Dive Bomber) Squadron, Seagrove, 1944.*

Below: *NZ5049 heading for a strike on Rabaul.*

Both photos official RNZAF via M. Laird

Mexican Air Force

By Santiago A. Flores

The Fuerza Aerea Mexicana (Mexican Air Force) received a total of 30 Douglas A-24B under the Lend Lease agreements between the USA and Mexico during World War II. They were supplied under requisition M-45 for 30 RA-24Bs; these were the only true combat aircraft that Mexico received during the war years from 1942 to1945, apart from training, transports and liaison aircraft.

Near the end of the war, they would receive 3 North American B-25J Mitchell medium bombers, and the 201st fighter squadron was operating the P-47D in the Pacific.

The subtypes delivered were as follows:
15 A-24B-1 DT
10 A-24B-10 D
5 A-24B-15 DT

Reportedly female WASP pilots flew the aircraft from the plant down to Texas for delivery. The aircraft were built at the Douglas-Tulsa Oklahoma Plant. They were delivered in 4-6 aircraft batches between June and November 1943. All aircraft were flown to the San Antonio Air Depot, and then picked up from Kelly Field Texas by Mexican pilots and flown to the military airbase of Balbuena, outside Mexico City

On their arrival the Mexican A-24Bs were assigned to Escuadron Aereo A-24 (Aerial Squadron A-24). Later in August 1944 Squadron 208 was formed with 22 A-24Bs, based in Mexico City. At first the Mexican A-24Bs received a Mexican AF serial number beginning with A- and the individual number of

Mexican A-24B dive bomber in flight over the Mexican countryside, possible after its delivery in 1943 either in service with Squadron 201 or Squadron 208 at Mexico City.
Ing. Enrique Velasco coll. via Santiago A.Flores

the aircraft as noted in some pilot log books, as per example that of SubTte P.A. Jacobo Estrada Luna:

Date	Type of AC	AC number	fight time	Reason
10 Sept. 1943	A-24	A-4	0.55	formation

Another pilot was SubTte P. A. Julio Cal y Mayor Sauz:

Date	Type of AC	AC number	fight time	Reason
1 Sept. 1943	A-24	A-4	2.10	formation

By October 1943 the A-24B received the Mexican designation BID "Bombardero Inclinado Douglas" (Dive Bomber Douglas), and Mexican AF serial numbers 2501 to 2530.

By the end of the year another unit was formed on the A-24B, Squadron 201 (Escuadron Aereo 201), that came into existence on December 1st 1943. Both Escuadron Aereo 208 and 201 were assigned to the 1st Military Zone (Zona Militar) in Mexico City. Based on the log book of Tte. P. A. Amador Samano Pina, who was assigned to Squadron 201 during the period of January to June 1944, the unit had the following A-24Bs on strength, along with North American AT-6 trainers.

12 A-24B: BID- 2504, 2506, 2507, 2508, 2509, 2510, 2512, 2516, 2521, 2525, 2526, 2529

2 AT-6: EAN-721 and EAN-736

Around 1943, two A-24Bs were sent to the Mexican Air force base at El Cipres, Ensenada Baja California, to Escuadron Aereo 202. This unit also had North American AT-6s, that were being used to patrol the Pacific coast.

Mexican A-24B. Note the American insignia under the Mexican one on the fuselage.
Ing. Enrique Velasco coll. via Santiago A.Flores

Mexican A-24B in flight somewhere over or near Mexico City, probably during the war years.
Ing. Enrique Velasco coll. via Santiago A.Flores

It has been repeated many times that the A-24Bs were used for anti-submarine patrols in the Gulf of Mexico. So far I have not found evidence to support this, only two A-24Bs were sent to the Baja California, and Squadron 201 and 208 were based in Mexico City.

Because of the arrival of these dive bombers, a group of Mexican pilots were sent to the Naval Air Station at North Island, San Diego California, for training. They arrived in February 1944, and they were provided with 8 USN SBD-5s, that were painted in Mexican markings. The aircraft received the following numbers (as mentioned in the unit's reports and pilot's log books): C-43, C-44, C-47 and C-48. This unit was organized by a USMC pilot, a veteran of Guadacanal, Lt. Col. Michael Sampas. This unit flew their last training missions early July 1944, the pilots were sent back to Mexico City. As for the aircraft, they were returned to the US Navy.

The Air order of Battle (AOB) shows the Mexican AF with the following A-24Bs in the following locations for June 1944

A-24B of Squadron 200 with the yellow cowling and yellow stripes on the wing, carrying a different version of "Casper the friendly ghost" insignia.
Ing. Enrique Velasco coll. via Santiago A.Flores

Mexican Air Force personnel at the USN air station of North Island, San Diego, discussing tactics with a USN pilot under the loaned SBD-5 to be used by the Mexican pilots in training. 1944.
Ing. Enrique Velasco coll. via Santiago A.Flores

Ensenada BC 4 A-24B*
Mexico City 22 A-24B

When the 201st left for the USA to convert to P-47s, another unit was formed to take their A-24Bs, this was Escuadron Aereo 209 (Squadron 209), that was also assigned to the 1st Military Zone at Mexico City.

After the end of the war the AOB of 24 May 1946 shows the following dispositions of the A-24B fleet:

EscuadronAereo 208	1/o. Grupo Aereo	17 A-24B 8 AT-6	Mexico City
Escuadron Aereo 209	1/o. Grupo Aereo	10 A-24B 8 AT-6	Mexico City
Escuadron Aereo 2022		A-24B 4 AT-6 1 AT-11 1 UC-61	Ensenada BC

As for Squadron 201, now flying the P-47D Thunderbolt, a training plan was established to train future fighter pilots. As the unit also served as a training unit, its inventory consisted not only of the P-47 but a number of AT-6s and A-24Bs.

When a new pilot joined the unit, he undertook a 50 hour training course that consisted of about 10 hours in the AT-6 and later five hours in the A-24B, with landings without using the flaps to simulate the landing speed of the P-47D. From the there the candidate would move to the P-47.

As for the post war years, the number of operational A-24Bs started to dwindle due to accidents and maintenance problems. For example Escuadron Aereo 209 during the period from June 1949 to October 1949 had about six A-24Bs operational.

By 1950 a British report (dated 19 January 1950) had the following A-24Bs listed: 8 serviceable, 7 unserviceable, 6 destroyed

AOB 31 March 1950
4/o.Grupo Aereo (4th Air Group) at Cozumel Q.R.
19 total A-24B
6 non-operational A-24B

Squadron 206 at Cozumel Q.R.
5 A-24B
1 Consolidated Model 21-M
3 Sikorsky OS2U Kingfishers
3 Stinson L-5E
3 B-25J Mitchell

Squadron 209 at Cozumel Q.R.
14 A-24B

As the number of operational A-24Bs went down, survivors were assigned to other units. By June 1956 4 A-24Bs were operational with Squadron 200, and by 1960 only two were left. One A-24B was reported operational with Squadron 202 in April 1961, with 3 AT-6s, but by 1962 the A-24s had been withdrawn from service after both units received new aircraft, in the form of the T-33, DH Vampire F.3 and the North American T-28A.

Side view of a silver overall A-24B in the post war years. The colour of the stripe is probably blue.
Ing. Enrique Velasco coll. via Santiago A.Flores

FAM serial	US serial	FAM serial	US serial	FAM serial	US serial
1	42-54316	11	42-54384	21	42-54576
2	42-54317	12	42-54385	22	42-54578
3	42-54318	13	42-54386	23	42-54573
4	42-54319	14	42-54387	24	42-54579
5	42-54320	15	42-54388	25	42-54581
6	42-54338	16	42-54489	26	42-54682
7	42-54339	17	42-54490	27	42-54680
8	42-54340	18	42-54491	28	42-54681
9	42-54341	19	42-54492	29	42-54683
10	42-54342	20	42-54493	30	42-54679

Middle: A silver A-24B used as a training aid at the Military aviation school of Mechanics in the post war years.

Bottom: A silver A-24B in flight. Note the details of the colour scheme.
Both photos: Ing. Enrique Velasco coll. via Santiago A.Flores

Chile

by Germán Lüer

Chile was another Latin American country to receive Banshees under Lend-Lease. Between June and August 1943 Chile took delivery of twelve A-24B-1-DT aircraft in four shipments. These were supplied to the Fuerza Aérea de Chile (FACh, Chilean Air Force) with three spare engines.

The aircraft were taken on charge by Grupo 4 of FACh, the unit based at El Bosque near Santiago, and later Grupo 4 had to relocate at Colina AFB, north of Santiago.

In Chile the A-24Bs were operated for a relatively short period. The last two A-24s in Chilean service (FACh 704 and 710) were phased out of service and struck off charge from Grupo de Aviación no. 6 based at Magallanes on 5 April 1950. This followed a request from Grupo 6 headquarters issued on March 20, due to the wing centre section stress and lack of spares to keep these aircraft in operation. The reason for this short operational time has its origins in the use of these attack bombers for a series of long-range flights for navigation training practices. One of these long-distance flights was made with the aim of covering the whole country from Punta Arenas to Iquique. These flights caused significant fatigue on the planes and this led to various accidents that forced the withdrawal of almost the entire fleet from service. The survivors were handed over to Grupo 6 at Punta Arenas, in Chilean Patagonia, finishing their days in that austral city.

A-24 FACh 705, probably at Colina AFB. This aircraft saw service in Grupo de Aviación N°4.

G. Lüer coll.

Above: *Banshees landed somewhere in southern Chile - probably Coyhaique, a fuel-stop place that was considered for one of the long-range flights of this aircraft in Chile. The square-shaped symbol below 712's cockpit is the blue badge of Commander in Chief of Flight.*
Below: *A-24 with FACh no 707 on the wing leading edge and the second number 347, which means that this aircraft had USAF serial 42-54347. Photo was taken inside the 'Hangar Junkers' located at El Bosque AFB. This hangar was built in the 1920s with the arrival of the Junkers R42 aircraft and it still exists today.*
Both photos G. Lüer coll.

CAC serial	US serial	CAC serial	US serial
701	42-54309	707	42-54347
702	42-54313	708	42-54389
703	42-54343	709	42-54390
704	42-54344	710	42-54391
705	42-54345	711	42-54392
706	42-54346	712	42-54393

Right: *FACh 701 and other Banshees during inspection at Colina AFB.*
Below: *An air-to-air shot of FACh 709 taken from aircraft no 707. The distinctive-shaped Chilean insignia is clearly visible..*
Both photos G. Lüer coll.

France

In early 1943 the reactivated Aeronavale (French navy air service) asked the USA to supply SBD-5s for the re-created naval aviation. The French reminded the Americans that back in June 1940 they had ordered 174 Dauntlesses that were never delivered. However, it took until autumn 1944 before 39 SBD-5s were delivered to Agadir in Morocco.

The aircraft were used to form two units: Flottiles 3B and 4B. Both the units fought in France, from December 1944, within the American First Tactical Air Force. The flew a total of 1,500 sorties in 1,426 combat hours and dropped some 500 tonnes of bombs. Losses amounted to five aircraft.

L'Armee de l'Air (the French air force) received 55 A-24s in two batches. The aircraft were supplied to the French in Morocco in the second half of 1943. The French asked for another 100 A-24s, but the Americans decided to provide A-35s.

Initially the A-24s were allocated to second line fighter units, but combat operations necessitated their move to the front line. French Banshees formed two dive bomber units: GB I/17 Picardie and GB I/18, each consisting of two 10-aircraft escadrilles. After training, GB I/17 Picardie was transferred to Syria and the rest of A-24s were used as advanced training aircraft.

In spring 1944 the A-24 joined GCB I/18 Vendee that was moved to central France. The A-24s flew against Wehrmacht units, often in support of Resistance formations. The unit ended operations on 18 April 1945.

As opposed to the RAF and USAAF, French pilots considered the A-24 an ideal aircraft for operations in Europe.

After the war French A-24s continued to serve in training units until 1953.

A-24B-DT, F 905, 1945.
J. Cuny coll.

A-24B-DT, F 906, 1945.
J. Cuny coll.

Nine French SBD-5s were loaded aboard the aircraft-carrier *Dixmude* (ex-HMS *Biter*). They were allocated to Flotille 3FB, subsequently renamed Flotille 3F. In January 1947 the unit sailed aboard *Dixmude* to Indochina, where communist guerrillas had risen against the French. From February until April 1947 the Dauntlesses flew combat operations against the Vietnamese forces, operating mainly from airfields in Tonkin, as the *Dixmude's* deck was too small and too dangerous for operations. After a period in Toulon (April to October 1947) *Dixmude*, with nine Dauntlesses of Flottile 4F, returned to Indochina in October 1947. Three Dauntlesses were despatched to Tonkin and the other six operated from Cochin-China. The SBD-5s took part in fighting in Central Annam, in the battle of Tan Son Nhut and on the Red River. The intensity of

SBD-5 of Flottile 3F, post war.
via J. Fernandez

Above: SBD-5 of Flottille 3F taking off.
***Below:** SBD-5 of Flottille 4F on Arromanches, Indochina 1947.*
via J. Fernandez

the fighting resulted in heavy wear of the aircraft, so that the last Dauntless combat missions were flown on 26 and 29 March 1948.

Ten more SBD-5s arrived on 29 November 1948 in the war zone aboard the new aircraft-carrier *Arromanches* with Flotille 4F. The first combat mission was flown by these Dauntlesses on 11 December 1948. Operations were flown mainly in Tonkin. They made a total of 66 sorties in 300 flying hours. Nine SBDs (one was lost in accident) returned to France aboard Arromanches in January 1949.

Until 1950 the Dauntlesses were used for advanced training, preparing pilots for aircraft-carrier operations.

Top: SBD-5 of Flottille 4F taxing.

Bottom: Another SBD-5 of Flottille 4F after a deck landing accident.
all photos via J. Fernandez.

Sources & Bibliography.

1. Dive and Torpedo Bombers, J.V. Mizrahi, Sentry books, 1967.
2. SBD Dauntless in action, Aircraft Number 64, Rob Stern, Squadron/Signal Publications, Carrollton,1984,
3. SBD Dauntless, in detail & scale, Bert Kinzey, Squadron/Signal Publications, Carrollton, 1996.
4. SBD Dauntless Units of WW2, Osprey Combat Aircraft 10, Barret Tillman, Osprey Publishing, 1998.
5. American Combat Planes, Third Enlarged Edition, Ray Wagner, Doubleday, 1982.
6. McDonnell Douglas Aircraft Since 1920: Volume 1, Rene J. Francillon, Naval Institute Press, 1988.
7. The Dauntless Dive Bomber of World War II, Barrett Tillman, Airlife, 1993.
8. Douglas TBD Devastator, SBD Dauntless, J. Ledwoch, J. Nowicki, Wydawnictwo Militaria, 2000.
9. Douglas SBD Dauntless, Peter C. Smith, Crowood Aviation Series, 1997.

Survivors list

Type	Dis-played as	BuNos Or US Serial	c/n	Current or civil Reg.	Status	Location
SBD-1	SBD-1	01612	565		Under Restoration	San Diego Aircraft Carrier Museum, CA
SBD-2	SBD-2	02106	-		Static Display	National Museum of Naval Aviation, Pensacola, Fl.
SBD-3	SBD-3	06624	2765	10715	Static Display	Kalamazoo Aviation History Museum, Kalamazoo, Mi
SBD-3	SBD-3	06626	B-24		In Store	National Museum of Naval Aviation, Pensacola, Fl.
SBD-3	SBD-3	06583			To Marine Corps	National Museum of Naval Aviation, Pensacola, Fl,
SBD-3	SBD-5	06508	1245		In Store	National Museum of Naval Aviation, Pensacola, Fl.
SBD-3	SBD-3	06694	1509		Static Display	USS Lexington Museum on the Bay, Corpus Christi, Tx.
SBD-3	SBD-3	10694	-		In Store	Courtesy Aircraft, Rockford, III.
SBD-4	SBD-4	06900	1775		Static Display	San Diego Aerospace Museum, San Diego, Ca.
SBD-4	SBD-4	06833	1708	-	Displayed as recovered	National Museum of Naval Aviation, Pensacola, Fl.
SBD-4	SBD-4	10518	2478	N4864J	Static Display	Yankee Air Corps, Chino, Cal.
SBD-4	SBD-4	10715			Under Restoration	Museum of Flying, Santa Monica, Ca
SBD-4	SBD-4	10828	2468	NZ5024	In Store	Greg Morris, Kansas
SBD-4	SBD-4	06853	1858	NZ5037	In Store	RNZAF Museum, Wigram AFB, NewZealand
SBD-4	A-24B	10575	2565		Static Display	Midway Airport, Chicago, IL
SBD-5	SBD-5	36173	04812		Static Display	USS Yorktown, Patriots' Point, Charlestone, S.C
SBD-5	SBD-5	36175	B-22		Static Display	Palm Springs Air Museum, Palm Springs, CA.
SBD-5	SBD-5	36177			In Store	National Museum of Naval Aviation, Pensacola, Fl.
SBD-5	SBD-5	28536	3883	N670AM	Airworthy	Planes of Fame Museum, Chino, Cal.
SBD-6	SBD-6	54605	6119	N54605	Static Display	National Air and Space Museum, Washington D.C
A-24A	SBD-3	42-60817	2350	N5254L 06583	Static Display	Tilamook Air Museum, Tilamook, OR
A-24B	SBD-3	42-54643	17482	N51382	Under Restoration	Fantasy of Flight, Polk City, Fl.
A-24B/ RA-24B	SBD-5	42-54593	17432	-	Under Restoration	Kevin R. Smith, Fredericksburg, Va.
A-24B-DE	SBD-5	42-54682	17521	NR93RW	Airworthy	Lone Star Flight Museum, Galveston, Tx.
A-24B-DE	SBD-5	42-54582	17421	N17421	Static Display	Loan to NMUSAF Wright Patterson, Dayton, OH.
A-24B		42-54654	17493		Under Restoration	Military Aircraft Restoration Corp., Long Beach, Cal.
A-24B	SBD-5	42-54532	6046	N54532	Under Restoration	MAPS Air Museum Akron OH.
A-24B	SBD-3	42-54654	17493		Under Restoration	MAPS Air Museum, North Canton, Ohio

Fuselage

Above: SBD-2 (Bu 02106) at the National Museum of Naval Aviation, Pensacola, Fl., USA
Below: SBD-5 (Bu 28536) at Planes of Fame Museum, Chino, California. Both photos J. Kightly

Above: *Rear of SBD-5 fuselage*
Below. *FFront view of SBD-2. BuNo 2106, which was land based at Pearl Harbor when the Japanese attacked on 7 December 1941. Transferred to VMSB-241 on Midway Island, the aircraft was one of sixteen squadron SBDs launched to attack the Japanese Fleet on 4 June 1942. Only half of this number would return, including BuNo 2106, which made a one-wheel landing on Midway scarred by 219 enemy bullet holes.*

Both photos J. Kightly.

Front view of SBD-4 at Yankee Air Corps Museum.
J. Kightly.

Close-up shot of SBD-2 nose.
J. Kigthly.

SBD-5, port side of the fuselage. Landing gear pivot and 75 gallon fuel tank are also visible in the port wing centre section..
A. Lochte.

Above: SBD-3.
Photo from Technical Manual..

***Right:** SBD-4. Forward part of the starboard fuselage. Wind deflector is extended..*

***Bottom:** Port side of SBD-5 fuselage. Rivet lines are visible.*
Photos A. Lochte.

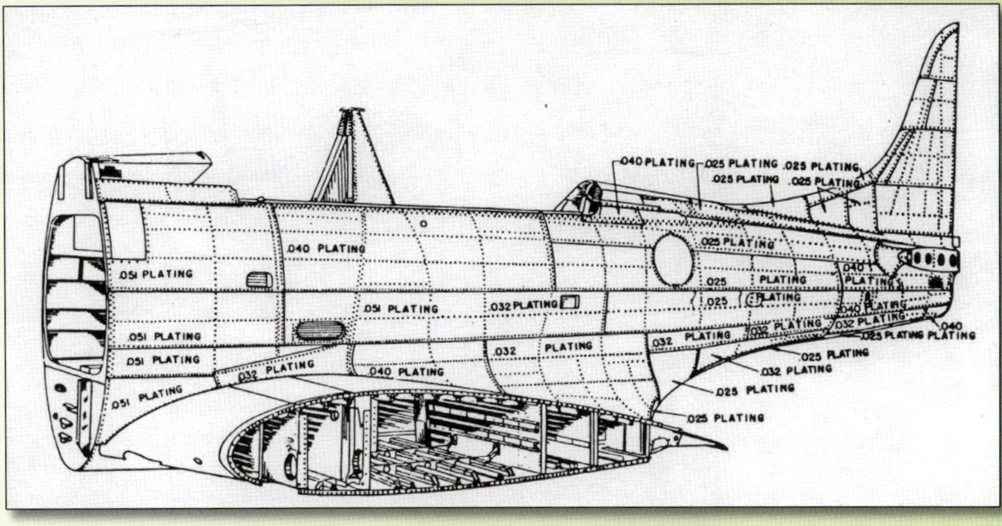

Above: Details of the fuselage skin thickness. Drawing from Technical Manual.

Left: The luggage compartment on the starboard side of the fuselage, in closed position in this photo.

Bottom. The luggage compartment in open position. Photos A. Lochte.

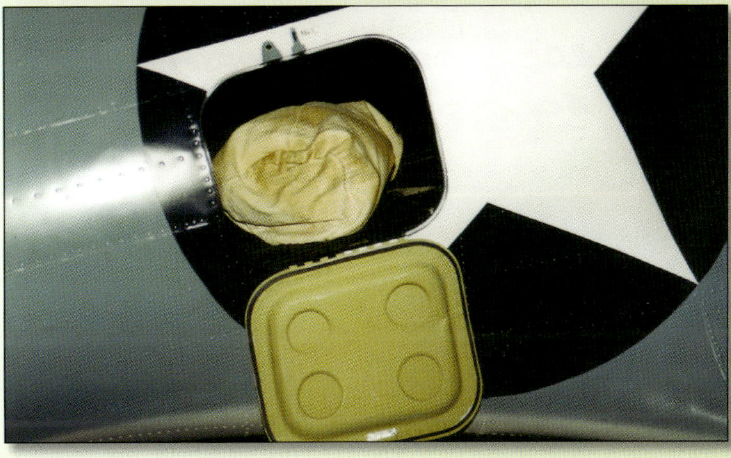

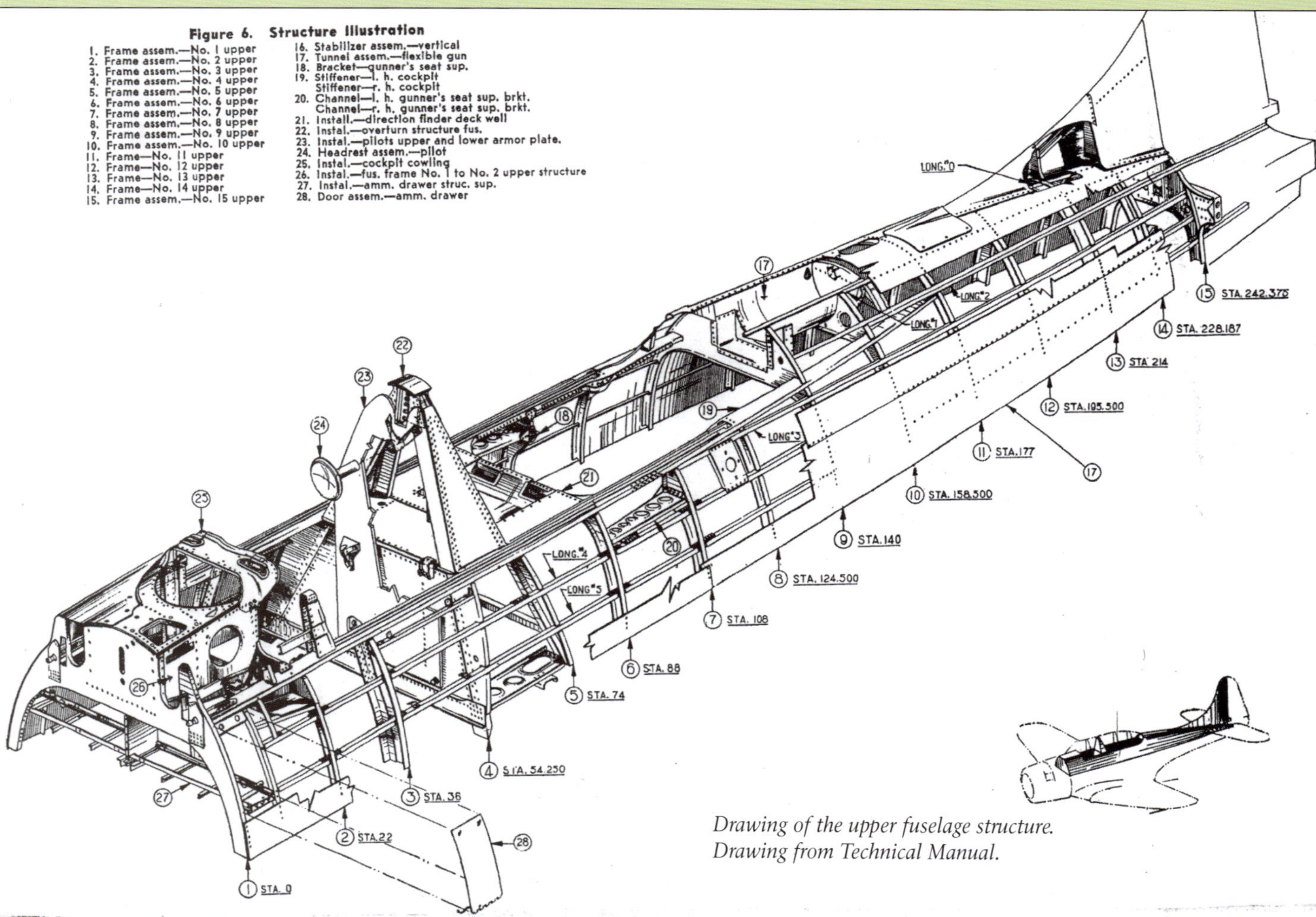

Drawing of the upper fuselage structure.
Drawing from Technical Manual.

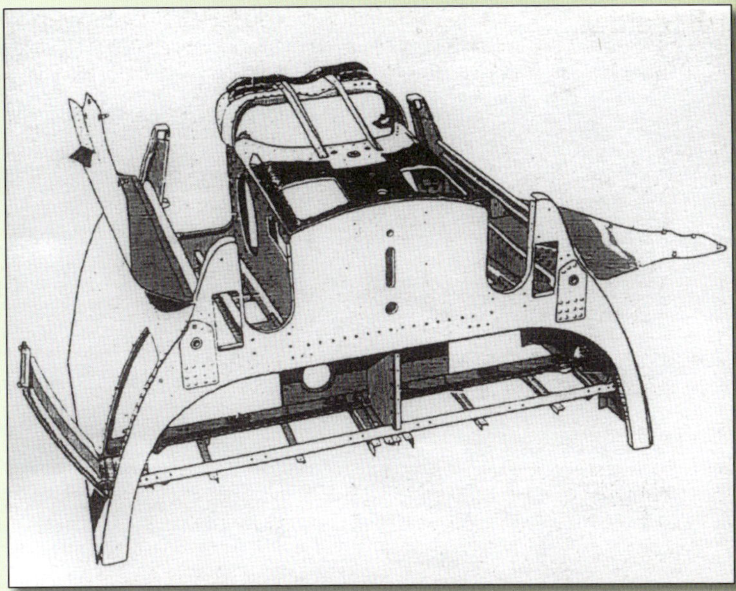

Left: *Details of the upper part of the fuselage, just in front of the cockpit. Drawing from Technical Manual.*

SBD-5; wooden antenna, cover to ammunition box and cockpit step are visible.

Port side of SBD-5 fuselage, just behind the cockpit.
Photos A. Lochte.

Above and bottom left: *Two lights, green (but looking blue when not illuminated) and clear, on the spine of the fuselage, just behind the cockpit.* ***Top, right:*** *Close up shot of the luggage compartment.* ***Right:*** *Door of the life-raft container on the port side of the fuselage. This door was hinged at the bottom.* ***Bottom, right:*** *Port side of SDB-5 during restoration. The overturn pylon is visible.*

All photos A. Lochte.

Above: *Starboard side of SDB-5 during restoration.*
Below: *Port side of the forward fuselage of SBD-4.*

Photos A. Lochte.

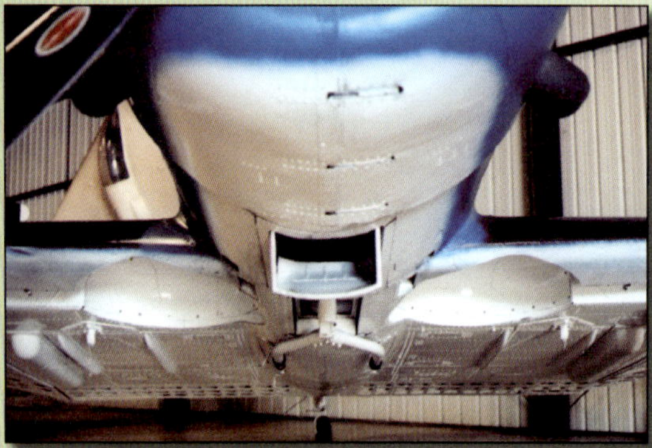

Top, left: *SBD-5, oil cooler scoop in open position. This scoop is located just in front of the bomb crutch.*
Above: *SBD-5. Hoisting point on port side of the fuselage.*
Above, right: *SBD-4 firewall, just in front of the cockpit, shown during restoration.*
Below: *Port side of SDB-5 fuselage during restoration. Life raft compartment door in open position.*

All photos A. Lochte.

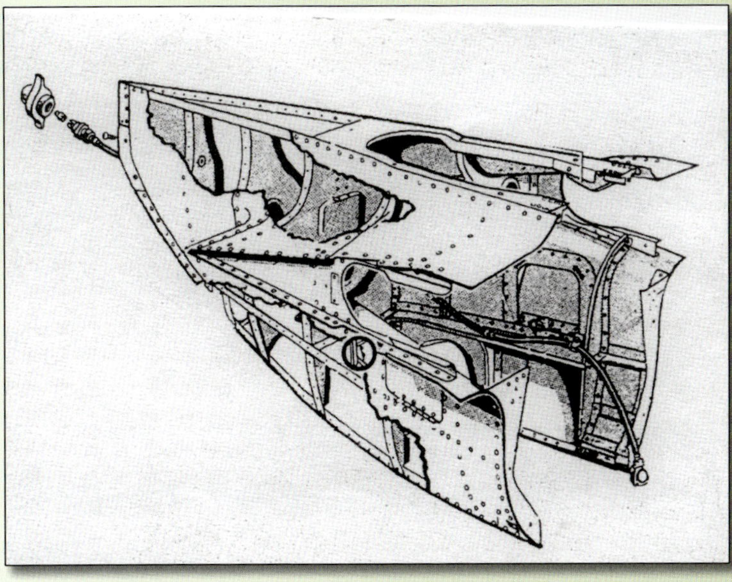

Tail cone assembly. Drawing from Technical Manual.

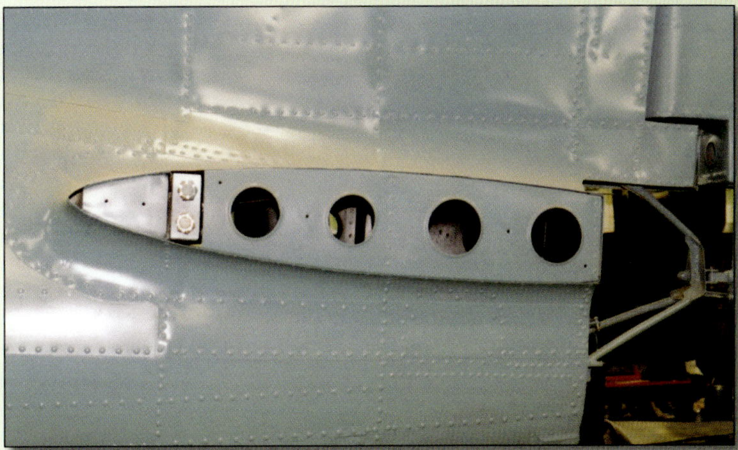

Two photos of the rear port side of the fuselage with stabiliser joint (upper) and rudder pivot (lower).

A. Lochte.

Two upper photos: *SBD-5. Port, rear part of the fuselage - doors to the two flare tubes. They were not present on A-24.*

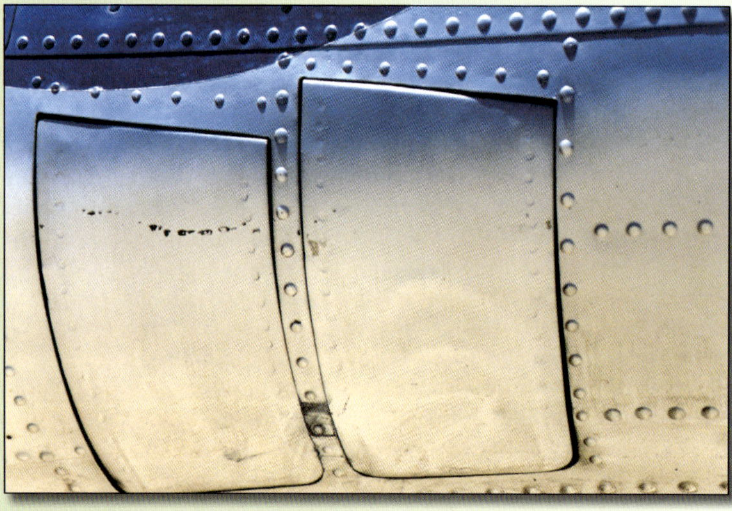

SBD-5, recessed area for centerline bomb covered by metal plate.
See also photos on page 110.

All photos A. Lochte.

Wing

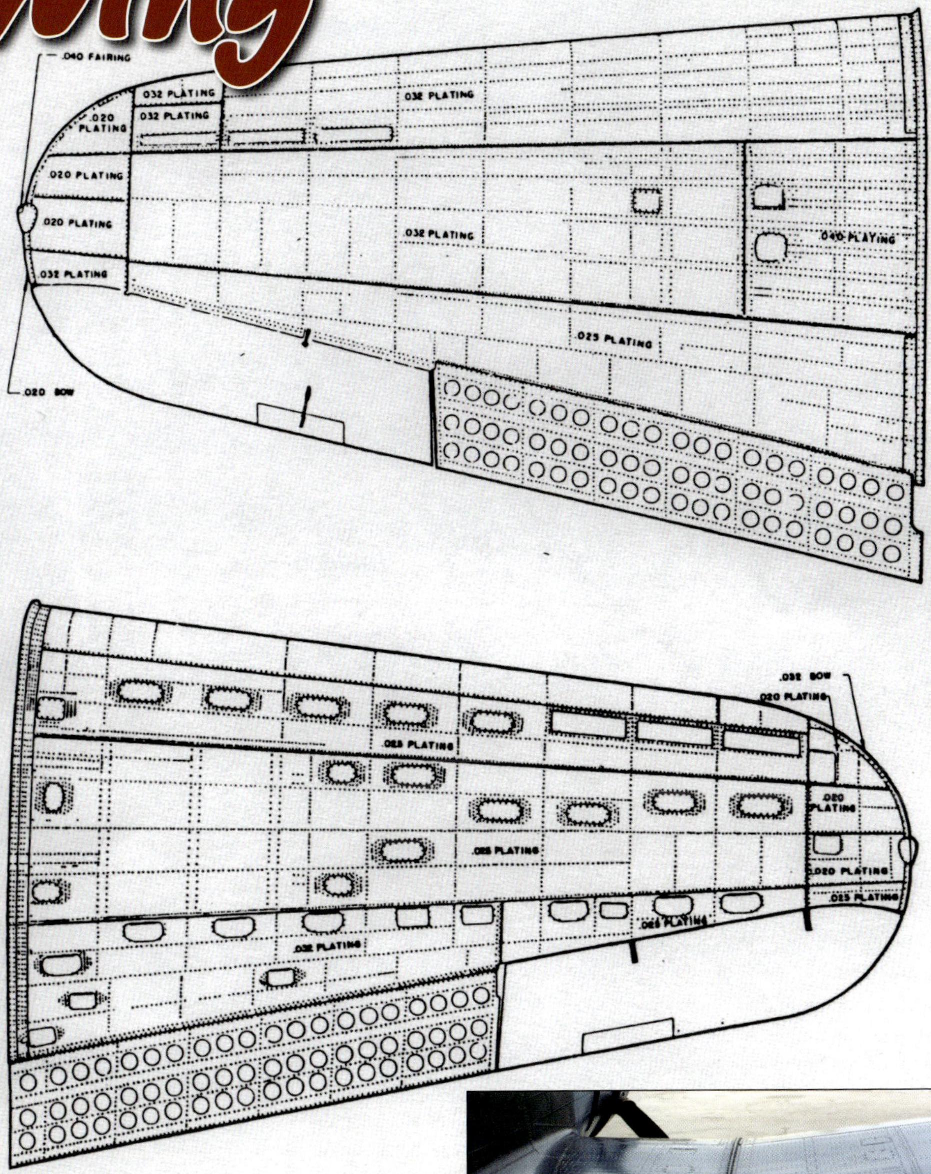

Above: *Drawings of the panels and rivet lines of the port wing. Note that retractable landing light is not shown. The panels and rivets on the starboard wing are the mirror image of the port one, excepting the trim tab on the flap. Drawing from Technical Manual.* **Right:** *Starboard wing, centre section. Note that fairing over wing joint is missing. A. Lochte.*

SBD-5, centre section of the port wing

Right: SBD-5, rivet detail of port centre section of the wing.
Below: Starboard aileron.
Photos A. Lochte.

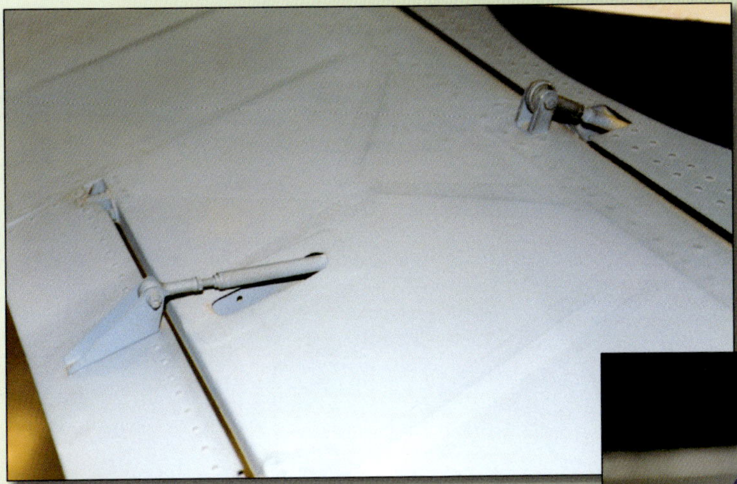

Left: SBD-4, Trim tab actuator on port aileron. Aileron control horn is also visible.

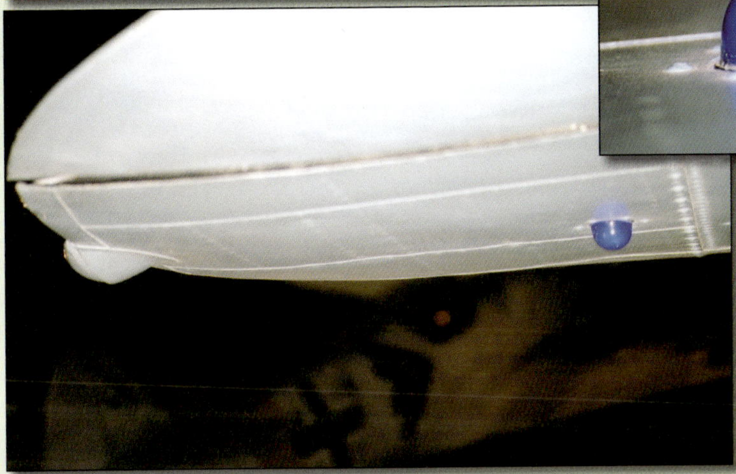

Above and left: *Photos of formation light.*

Bottom left: *Two photos of the navigation lights.*

Bottom right: *Underside of the port aileron.*

All photos A. Lochte.

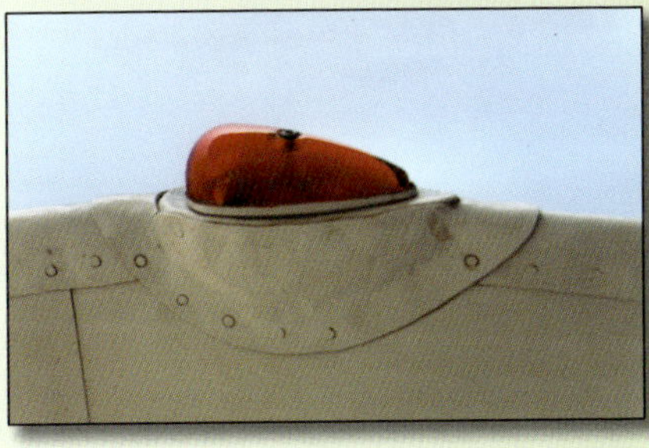

Above: *Port wingtip. Three slots are also visible.*
Middle: *Close-up shot of aileron control horn.*

Bottom: *Aileron hinge.*
All photos A. Lochte.

Above: *Tie-down ring cover on starboard wing tip.*

Left: *Tie-down ring in extended position.*

Left: *Bottom of the fuselage, wing intersection. Identification lights are visible. Red - forward, green - middle, amber - rear. Note, that antenna is a post-war addition.*

All photos A. Lochte.

Above: Three photos of port wing leading edge with landing attitude indicator lights.

Opening of the cockpit air intake.

Underside of the starboard wing.

All photos A. Lochte.

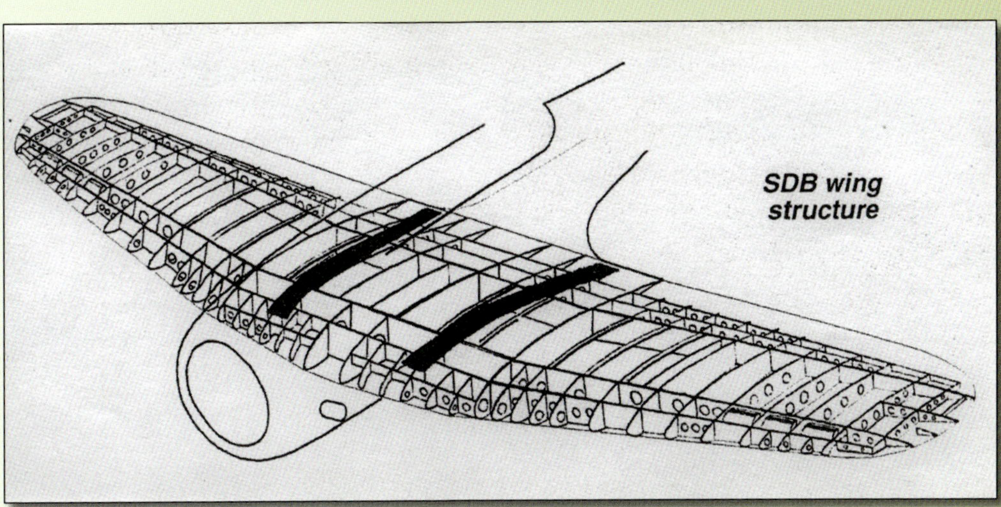

Above: Details of the wing structure.
Drawing from Technical Manual.
Middle: *Underside of the starboard wing during restoration. Note the numerous access panels in open position.*

Bottom: *SBD "Letter Box" fixed wing slots, underside of the port wing.*
All photos A. Lochte.

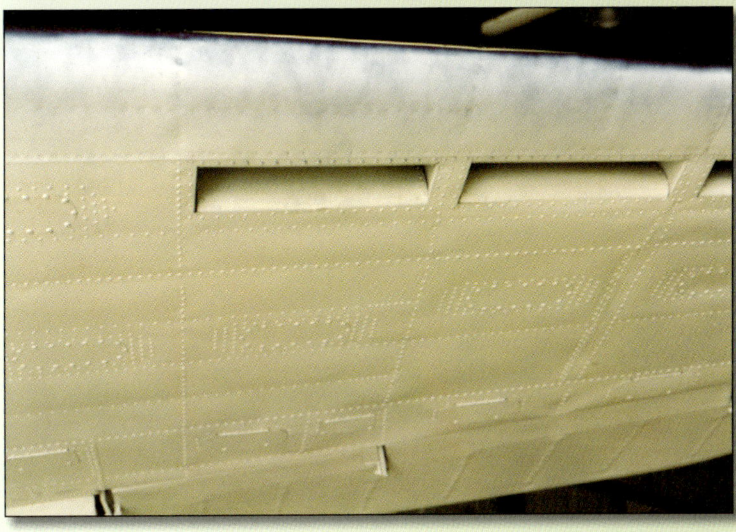

Above: *Upper surfaces of the port wing during restoration.*
Below: *Undersurface of the port wing tip.*

A. Lochte.

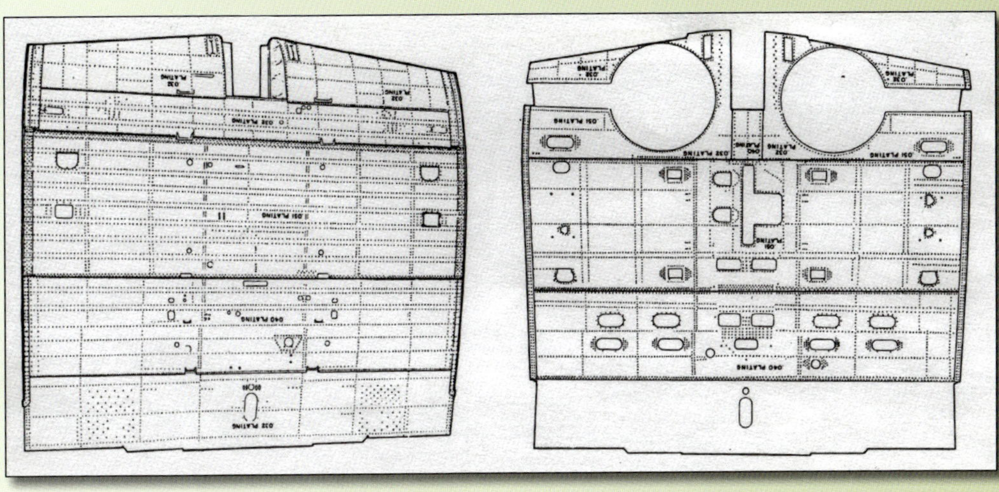

Above: *Top and underside of the centre wing section. Note that fairings and catapult hooks are deleted from drawings to show only plating, rivets and panels.*

Drawing from Technical Manual.

Middle and bottom: *Two photos of SBD-5, bottom of the port wing. Skin stiffeners are visible. Note also the catapult hook in the upper photo.*

Photos A. Lochte.

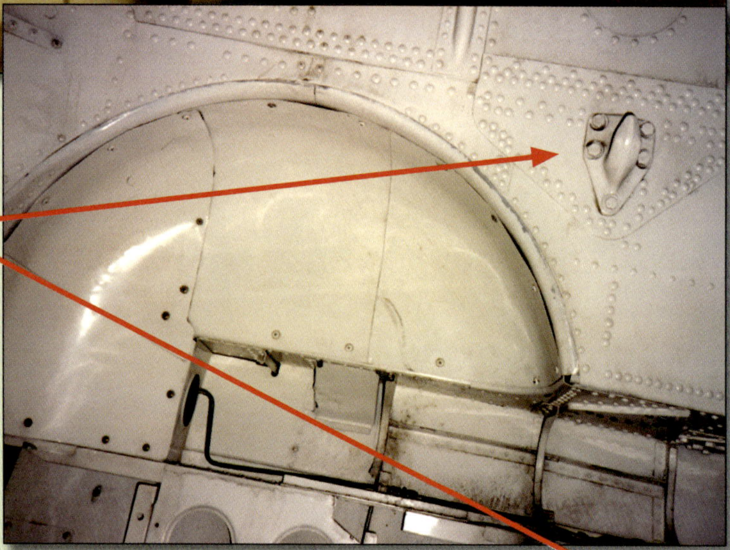

Above: *Bottom of the centre wing section.*

Right: *Catapult hook.*

Below, left: *Landing light in the retracted position, port wing.*

Below, right: *Bottom of the starboard wing centre section.*

All photos A. Lochte.

Dive Brakes

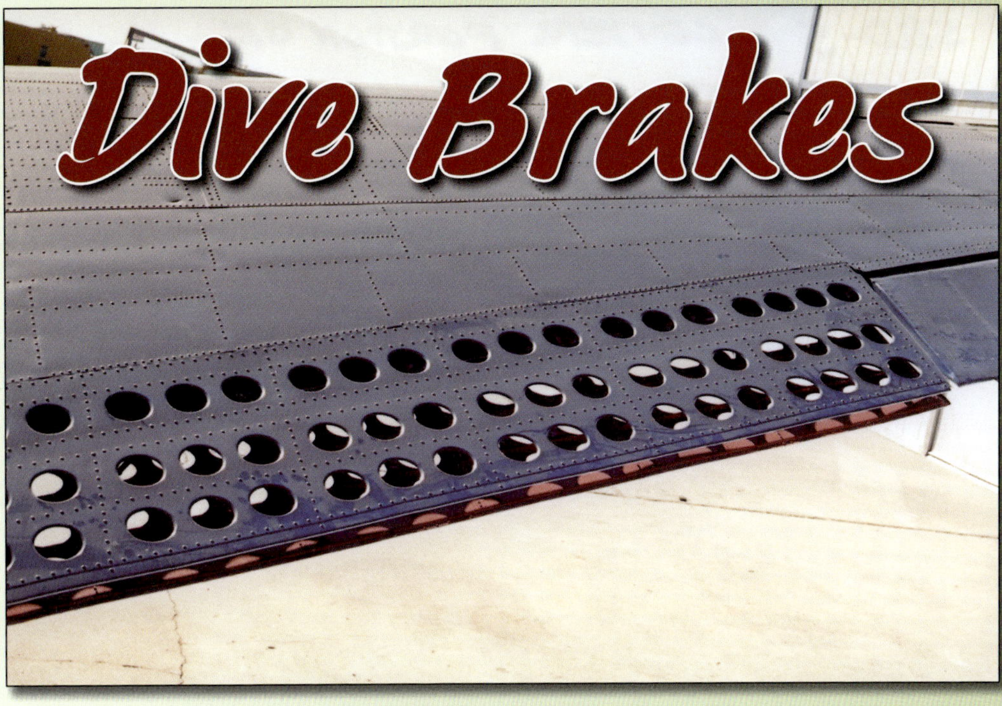

Above: *Uppersurface of the starboard dive brake in closed position.*
Below: *: Details of the holes in the dive brakes. Note that holes in the upper flap do not line up with the holes in the lower flap. A. Lochte.*

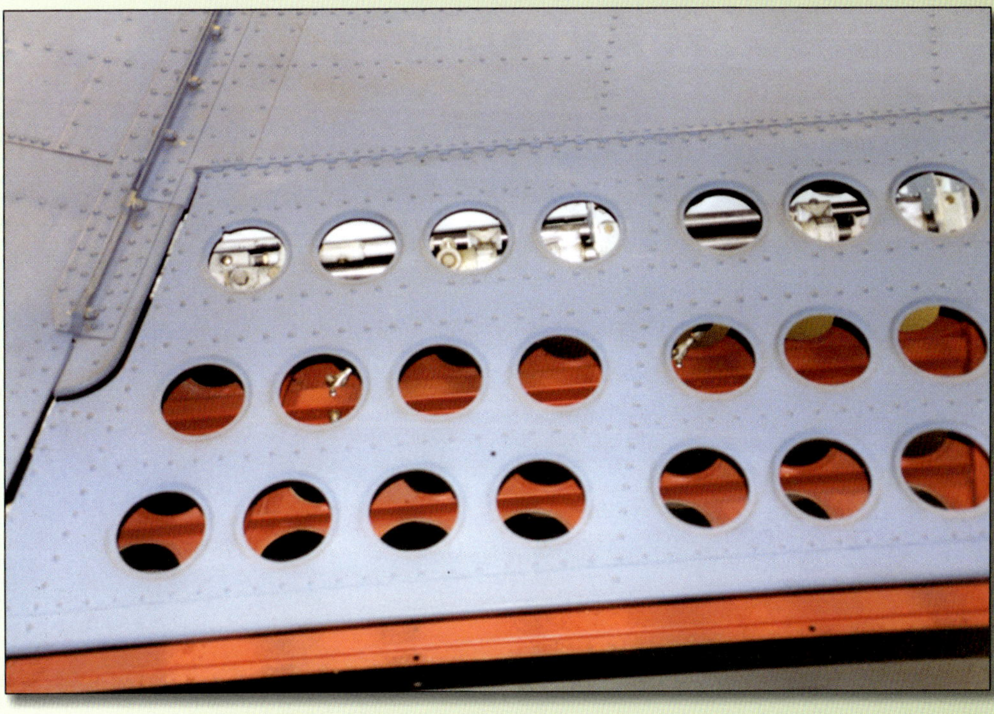

Top: *SBD-5, port wing, flaps in open position.*

Middle: *Details of the upper. port flap.*

Bottom: *Flap under centre wing and fuselage in open position.*

All photos A. Lochte.

This page: *Photos of the dive brake actuators. The interior of the flaps are painted in red, actuating rods are natural metal, areas between the rods and flaps are white.*

A. Lochte.

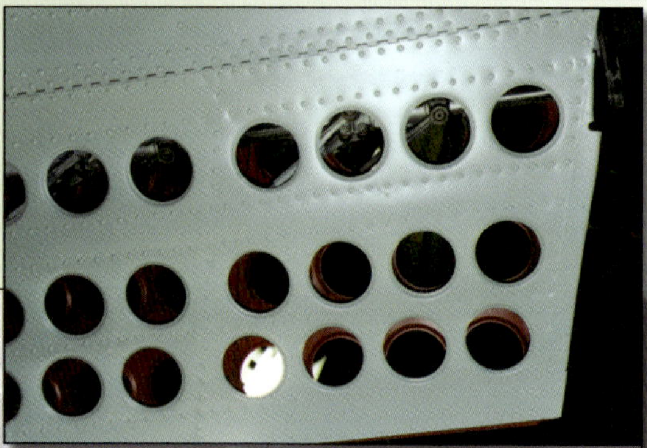

Above: *Details of the inner part of the flaps.*
Middle: *Holes and riveting of the bottom of the starboard dive brake.*
Bottom: *Outer view of the dive brakes.*

A. Lochte.

Engine

Above: *SBD-4, Wright R-1820-52 engine.*
Below: *SBD-4, engine cowling. A. Lochte.*

This page:
Top: *SBD-2 engine cowling, starboard side.*

Bottom: *Port side of the SBD-2 engine cowling.*
J. Kightly.

Opposite page.
SBD-4.
Details of engine equipment.
Engine mounting frames are also visible.
The green and yellow tank in the photos is for oil.
A. Lochte.

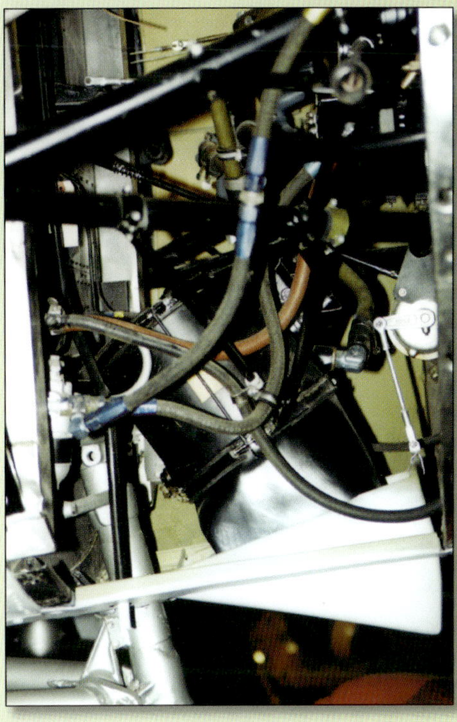

SBD-5, bottom of the cowling, port side. Oil cooler air scoop in open position. The hinged cover is for the fuel drain. The large rectangular opening is for spent shell casings.

***Right:** SBD-3, carburettor intake scoop. This scoop was similar in size on SBD-2, 3 & 4.*

***Bottom, right:** SBD-5, top of the cowling, port side. Cooling flap in open position.*

***Bottom, left:** SBD-5, cowling details from rear. Exhaust pipe is also visible.*

Photos A. Lochte.

Above: *SBD-5, propeller markings.*

A. Lochte.

Above: *Front view of SDB-5 cowling. Note that SBD-5 & 6 have no carburettor intake scoop. A. Lochte.*
Below: *SBD-1 engine details, , as recovered from Lake Michigan and displayed at the USNAM Pensacola. J. Kightly.*

Inner view of the engine cowlings.
Drawing from Technical Manual.

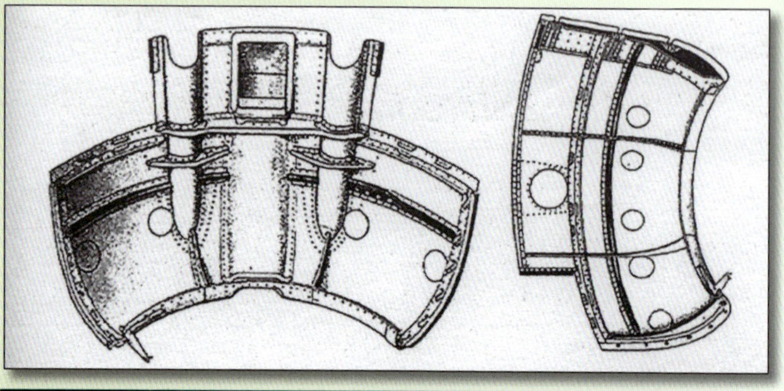

Two photos of SBD-3, upper engine cowling.
A. Lochte.

Two photos of exhaust pipe.

Bottom: *SBD-5, front view of bottom of the engine cowling. Oil cooling scoop in fully open position is also visible.*

A. Lochte.

Starter crank opening, starboard side.

Canopy & Cockpit

This page: SBD-5 canopy, starboard side. A. Lochte.

SBD-5 canopy, in open position, from the rear. The canopy of all Dauntless variants consisted of five pieces, two were fixed and three were movable.

Rear part of the SDB-5 canopy in closed position.
All photos A. Lochte.

Top & middle: *Two photos of the aft part of the canopy in closed position. Note the rubber strip around the rear framework.*

Starboard side of the pilot's sliding canopy.
All photos A. Lochte.

Starboard side of the rear 3 canopy sections.

The overturn pylon is an integral part of the fuselage structure.

Port side of the pilot's sliding canopy.
All photos A. Lochte.

Photos of canopy details A. Lochte.

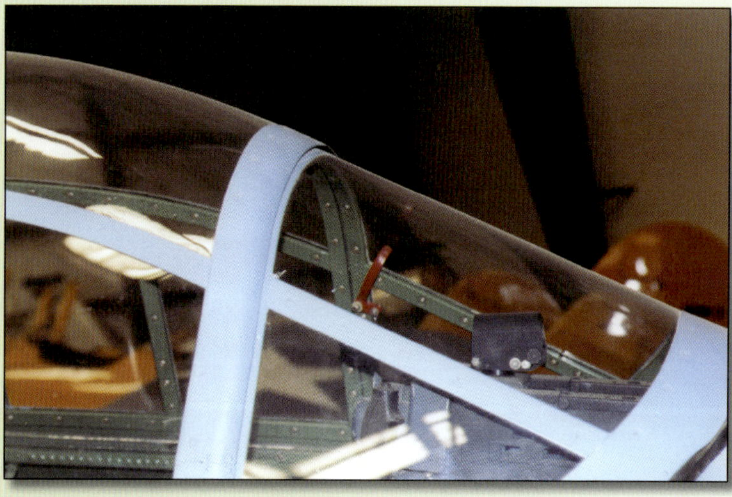

***Above and left**: SBD-3 instrument panel. Telescopic sight is also visible.*
***Below**: Pilot's bombing window in the bottom of the fuselage.*
***Bottom, left**. Canopy with overturn structure.*
All photos A. Lochte.

Front cockpit, upper view.
1. *Seat adjustment lever*
2. *Chartboard*
3. *Hoisting sling*
4. *Bombing aiming observation window*
5. *Safety belt*

Photo from Pilot's Manual.

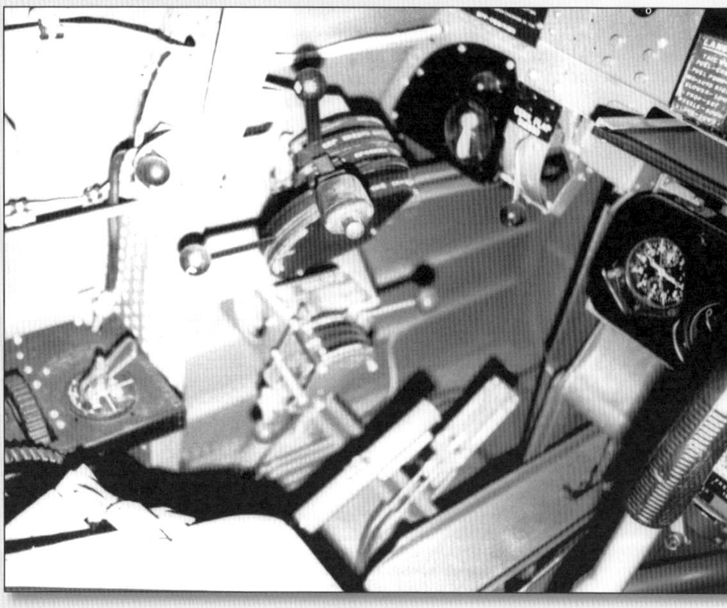

Front cockpit, port side.
A. Lochte.

SBD-3 Front Instrument panel.
1 . Airspeed indicator
2. Turn and bank indicator
3. Rate of climb indicator
4. Altimeter
5. Directional gyro control unit
6. Bank and climb control unit
7. Check-off instrument
8. Engine gauge unit
9. Manifold pressure gauge
10. Tachometer
11. Clock (elapsed time)
12. Engine temperature gauge
13. Outside air thermometer
14. Auto pilot pressure gauge
15. Fuel quantity gauges
Photo from Pilot's Manual.

SBD-3, SBD-3, lower instrument panel, engine instruments, rudder pedals and control column.
A. Lochte.

1. Control column
2. Carburettor air control
3. Cowling flap control lever
4. Auto-pilot on-off switch
5. Parking brake handle
6. Trigger switch
7. Cockpit ventilation
8. Engine primer
9. Oil coller air scoop cntrol
10. Ignition switch
11. Starter mesching pull
12. Windshield hot air control.
Photo from Pilot's Manual.

SBD-3 front cockpit looking forward through windscreen, compass at the top and telescopic sight are visible.

A. Lochte.

Front cockpit, port side.
1. *Blower control*
2. *Throttle*
3. *Mixture control*
4. *Propeller control*
5. *Bomb release lever*
6. *Bomb arming lever*
7. *Arrestor hook operating lever*
8. *Wobble pump handle*
9. *Fuel tank selector valve*
10. *Aileron tab control.*
I i. *Elevator tab control*
12. *Rudder tab control*
13. *Parachute flare release*
14. *Fire extinguisher release*
15. *Tail wheel lock*
16. *Landing gear position indicator*

Photo from Pilot's Manual.

Above: *front cockpit, starboard side.*
1. *Headrest release*
2. *Engine hydraulic pump control*
3. *Landing gear emergency lowering valve*
4. *Landing flaps selector lever*
5. *Flap position indicator*
6. *Dive brakes selector lever*
7. *Landing gear selector lever*
8. *Hand hydraulic pump*
9. *Very pistol bracket*
10. *Distribution panel*
11. *Fuse panel*
12. *Oxygen rebreather racks*
13. *Rounds counter*

Photo from Pilot's Manual.

Pilot's headrest.
1. Pilot's enclosure latch
2. Flotation manual release
3. Headrest
Photo from Pilot's Manual.

Gunner's sliding canopy in closed position, starboard side.
A. Lochte.

Front cockpit floor.
1. Rudder pedals
2. Brake pedals
3. Rudder pedal adjustment
4. Cockpit ventilator
5. Oil cooler air scoop operating lever
6. Control surfaces lock
7. Brake pedal adjustment
Photo from Pilot's Manual.

SBD-3, front cockpit, control column.
A. Lochte.

Above: *Rear cockpit, looking forward.*
1. Rudder pedal adjustment
2. Removable control column

Above, right: *Rear cockpit, upper view.*
Photo from Pilot's Manual..

Starboard side of the middle section of the canopy.
A. Lochte.

Rear cockpit, looking forward.
1. Airspeed indicator
2. Clock
3. Altimeter
4. Switch panel
5. Lateral inclinometer
6. Flotation pull
7. Compass
6. Enclosure latch
Photo from Pilot's Manual.

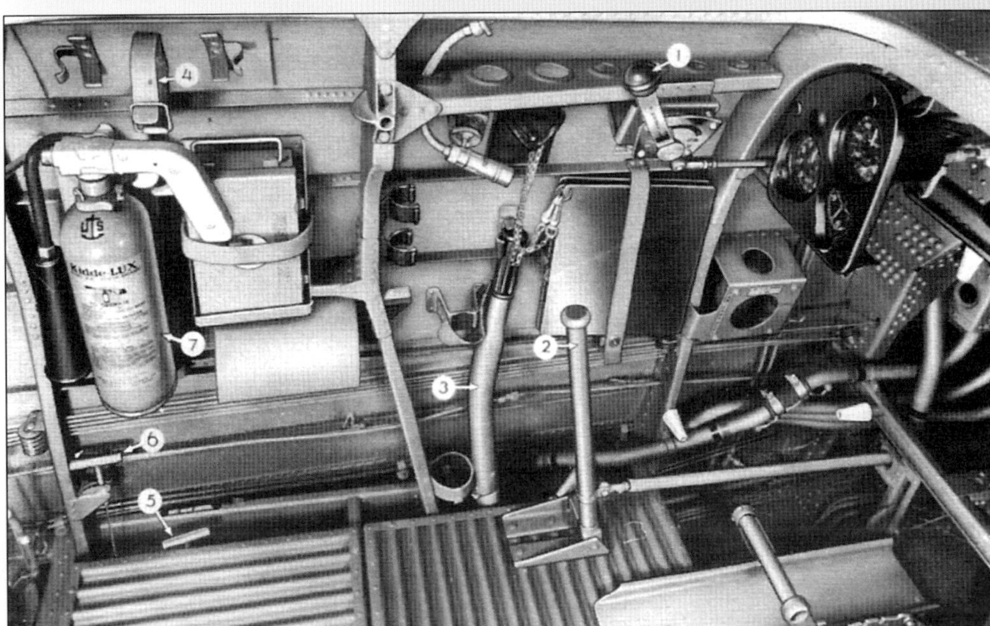

Bottom:
Rear cockpit, port side wall.
1. Throttle
2. Wobble pump handle
3. Control column (stowed)
4. Smoke grenade rack
5. Gate valve control
6. Tail pipe control
7. Hand fire extinguisher
Photo from Pilot's Manual.

Above: Rear cockpit, starboard sidewall.

1. Smoke grenade rack
2. Drift sight cutout
3. Oxygen rebreather racks

Right: Rear cockpit, rear wall.

1. Ammunition racks
2. Smoke grenade handle
3. Gun tunnel door release
4. Co_2 fire extinguisher bottle
5. Flotation system bottle
6. Float light racks

Photos from Pilot's Manual.

Tail

Above: Port side of the SBD-2 tail. Lighter worn panels are original, and unrestored. Also see page 99. J. Kightly.
Below: Starboard horizontal stabiliser, SBD-5. A. Lochte.

Top: Two photos of starboard elevator.

***Bottom, right:** Port horizontal stabiliser and elevator.*

***Bottom, left:** Details of stabiliser-fuselage intersection.*

All photos A. Lochte.

Details of the port elevator and trim tab.
A. Lochte.

Fairing of the fin - fuselage intersection.
J. Kightly.

Lower part of the tail cone.
A. Lochte.

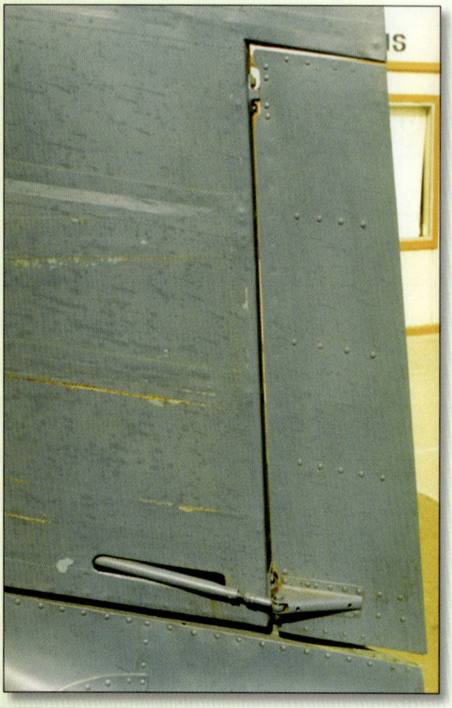

Details of the fin and rudder.
A. Lochte.

Undercarriage

Above: *General arrangement of the main undercarriage, SBD-5.*
Below: *Tail wheel, as used on A-24 and land-based SBDs, and arrestor hook. A. Lochte.*

Details of the main undercarriage. A. Lochte.

Details of the main undercarriage cover. Note inward angle to main oleo leg. A. Lochte.

Front view of the main undercarriage leg. Note that there is only one door for each main gear, and it covers only the main leg when gear is retracted.

A. Lochte.

A main wheel. Note that wheel is a spoked design but was almost always covered by a flat metal plate (see page 103).

A. Lochte.

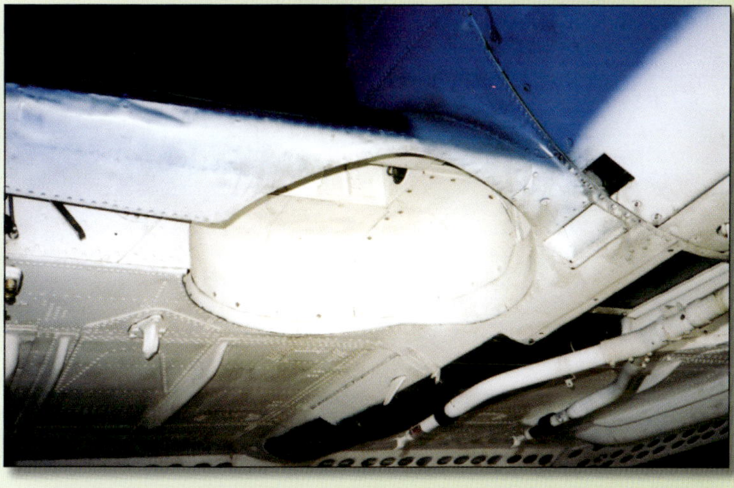

Three photos showing the main undercarriage well.
A. Lochte.

More views of the wheel well.

A. Lochte.

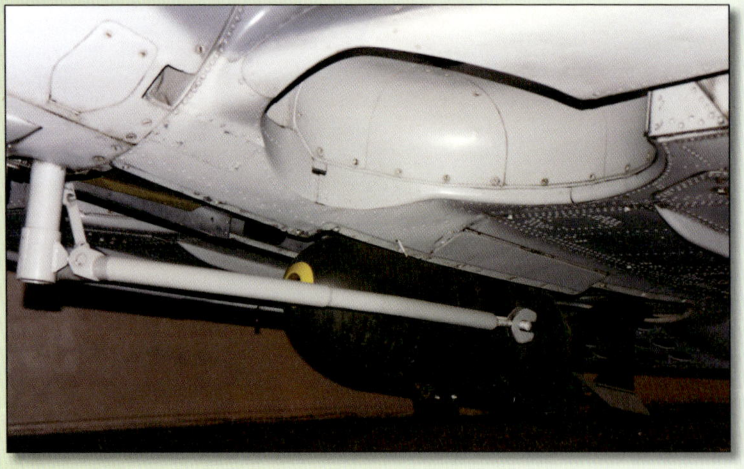

Photos of tail wheel as used on carrier-based SBDs.
The tow bar is also visible.

A. Lochte.

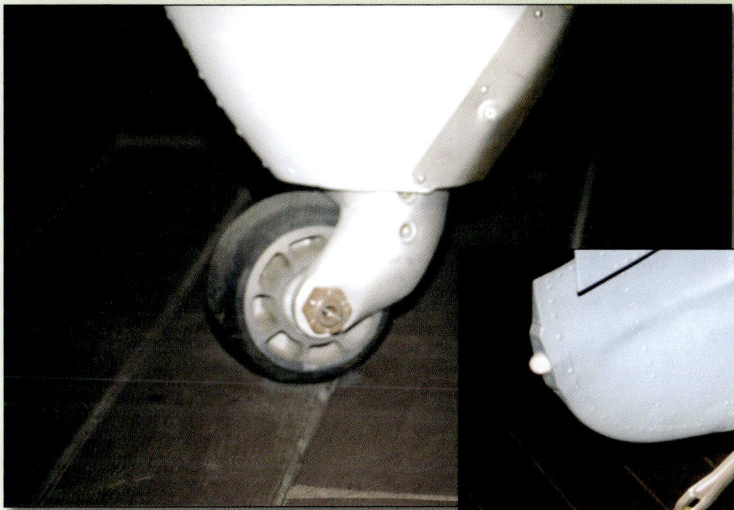

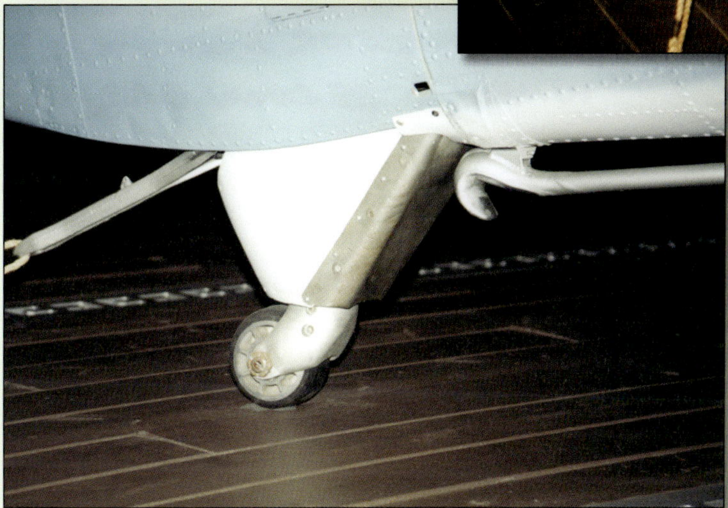

Photos of tail wheel as used on A-24 Banshees and land-based Dauntlesses. Arrestor hook is also visible.

A. Lochte.

Armament

Above: 1,000 pound bomb mounted on the centreline station.
Below: 1,000 pound GP bomb. A. Lochte.

Photos showing the centerline station.
A. Lochte.

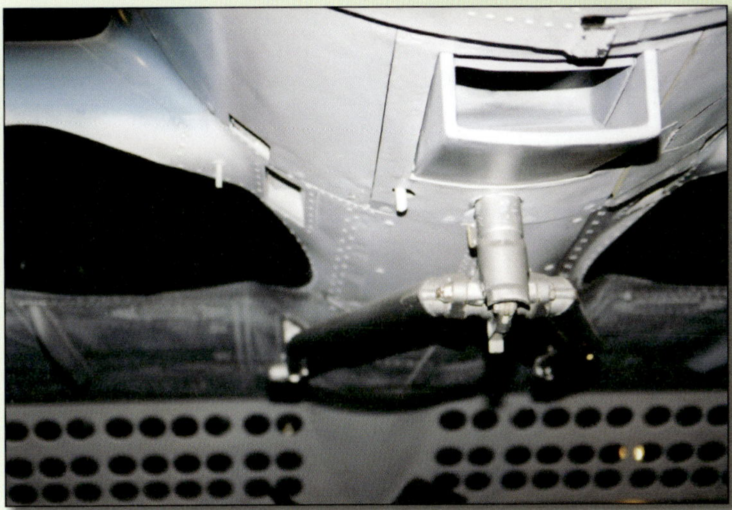

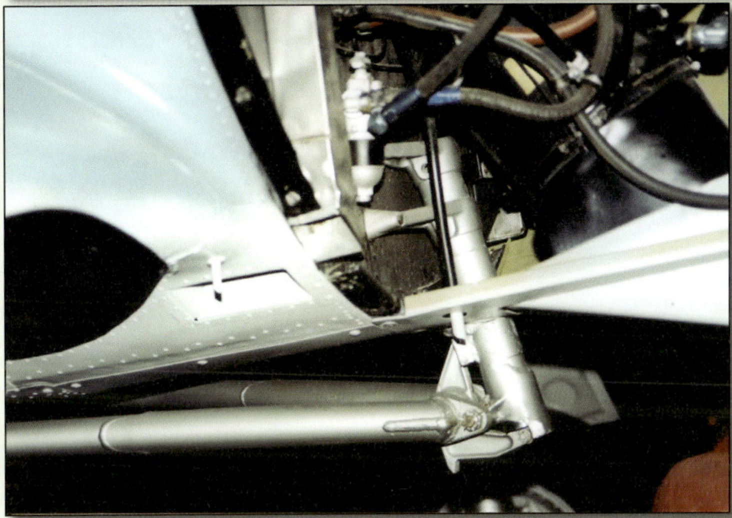

SBD-4. Two photos of the bomb crutch support. In the middle photo, the panels are removed showing bomb crutch support and pivot.

A. Lochte.

1,000 pound GP bomb type AN-M65. Bomb weight is 997 lb including 530 lb of explosive.

A. Lochte.

Close-up photo of 1,000 pound GP bomb and its fuses.

A. Lochte.

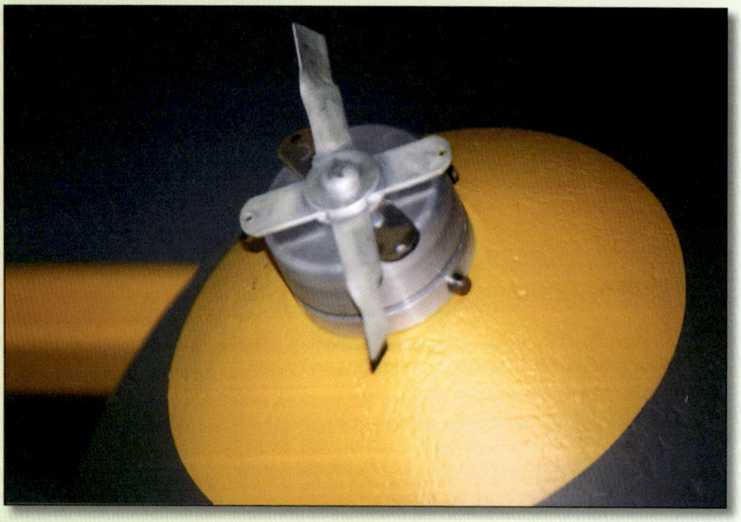

Photos of 100 lb bomb carried on bomb racks under the wings.
On the SBD-5 and SBD-6, external fuel tanks could be carried under the wings.
A. Lochte.

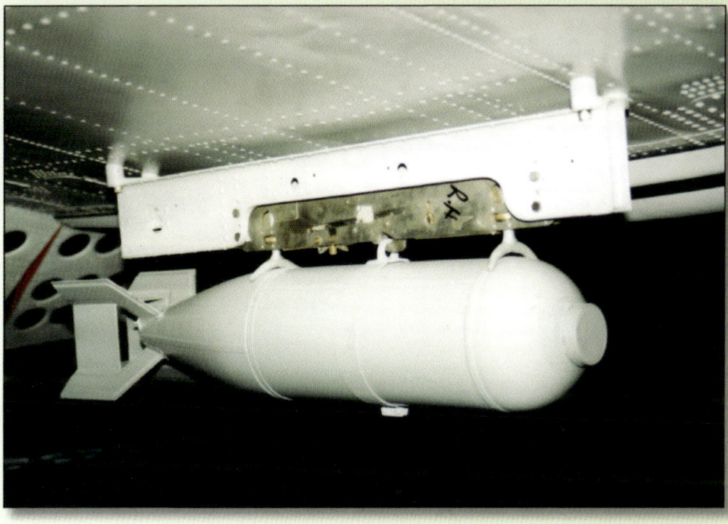

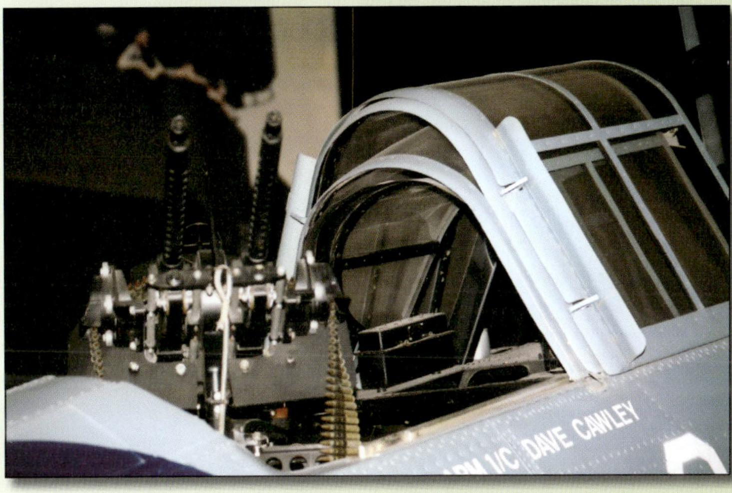

This page:
Photos of twin flexible gun mount.
The twin mount was two .30 caliber machine guns joined by a metal framework.
A. Lochte.

Opposite page:
A single mount as used on SDB-1, SBD-2 and early SBD-3.
J. Kightly.

Above: *SBD-5, side view of the twin mount.*
Middle and bottom left: *Two photos of the fixed gun ammunition boxes. A. Lochte.*
Bottom right: *Pilot's gun system. Drawing from Technical Manual.*

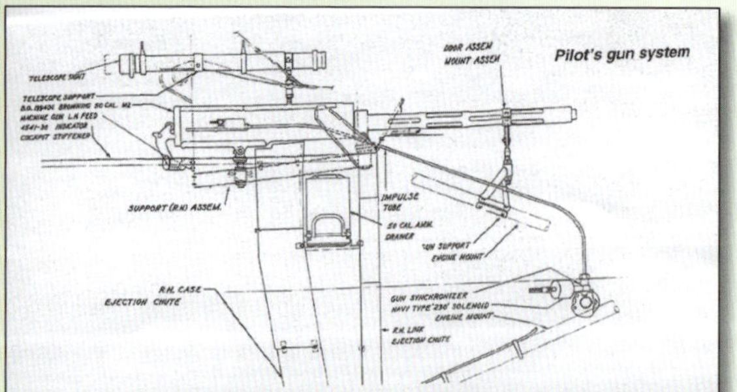

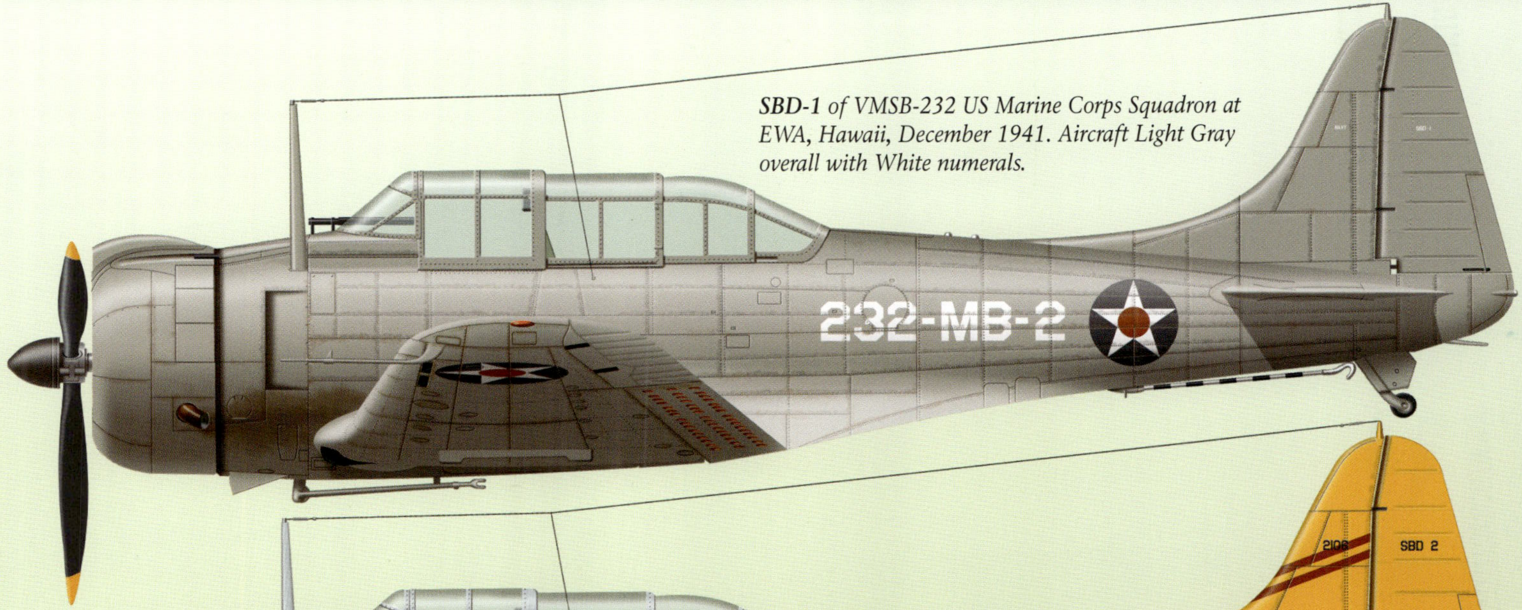

SBD-1 *of VMSB-232 US Marine Corps Squadron at EWA, Hawaii, December 1941. Aircraft Light Gray overall with White numerals.*

SBD-2, *BuNo 2108 of VMB-2, 1940. Overall Silver with Chrome Yellow wings and tail.*

SBD-2 BuNo 1616 of VMB-1, 11th Group at Quantico. Overall Silver with Chrome Yellow wings, Blue tail and fuselage bands.

This page and opposite page lower:
***SBD-1**, BuNo 1626, Sqn Commander's personal aircraft. VMB-2 US Marine Corps Squadron, Quantico, Virginia, USA, 1940. Overall Silver with Chrome Yellow wings, Red tail and fuselage bands.*

SBD-2 *of VMSB-241. Blue Gray upper surfaces with Light Gray lower surfaces.*

SBD-3 *of Bombing Six, USS Enterprise (CV 6), August 1942. Flown by Ens Robert C. Shaw and AO2/c Harold L. Jones.*

SBD-3 *of Bomber Eight (VB-8) from USS Hornet (CV 8), 1942*

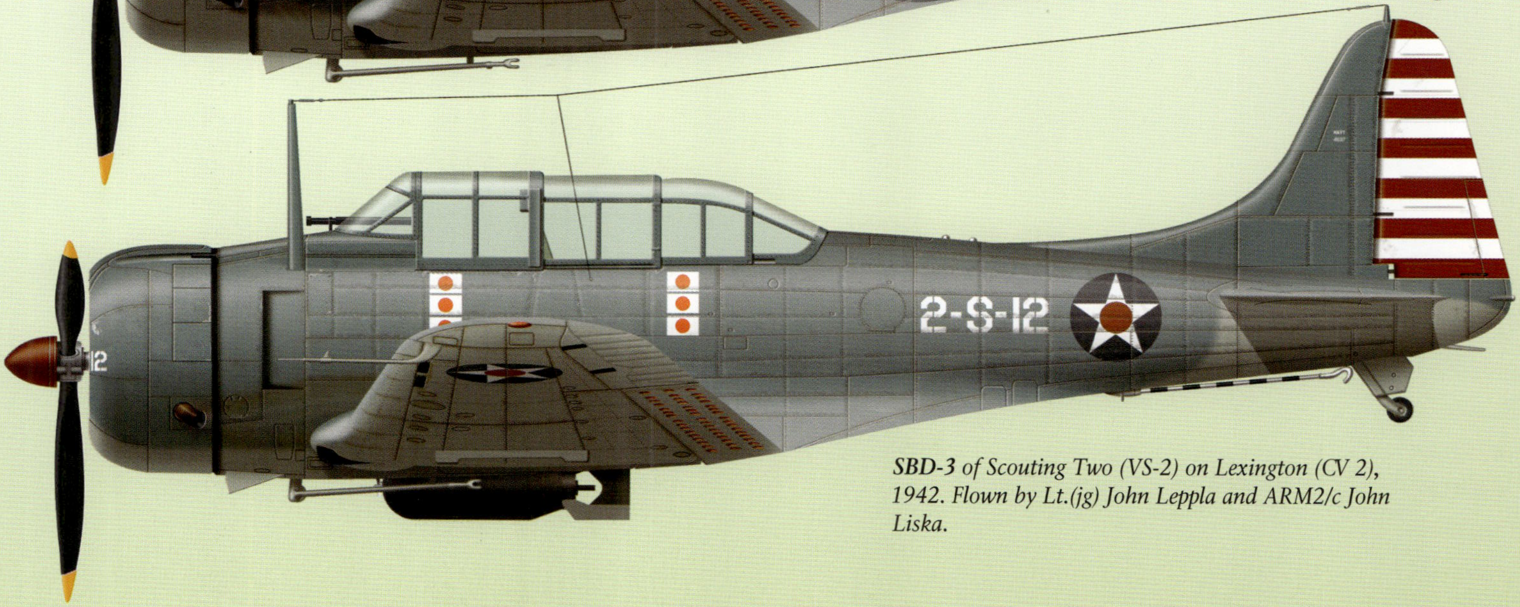

SBD-3 *of Scouting Two (VS-2) on Lexington (CV 2), 1942. Flown by Lt.(jg) John Leppla and ARM2/c John Liska.*

SBD-3, *BuNo 4537 of Scouting Two (VS-2) on USS Lexington (CV 2), 8 May 1942. Flown b y Lt(jg) William E. Hall and Seaman 1st Class John A. Moore.*

SBD-3 *of VS-41 from USS Ranger during Operation "Torch", November 1942.*

SBD-3 *BuNo 03213 on USS Saratoga (CV 3), August 1942. Flown by Cdr Harry D. Felt and Chief Radioman Cletus A. Snyder.*

SBD-3 *of Bombing Three (VB-3) on USS Saratoga (CV 3), August 1942. Flown by Lt(jg) Robert M Elder and Radioman 2nd Class L. A. Till.*

SBD-4 of VMSB-144, Solomon Islands, November 1943. Flown by Maj Frank E. Hollar

SBD-5 *of Bombing Nine (VB-9) on USS Essex (CV 9), Rabaul, November 1943. Top of fuselage - Non Specular Sea Blue ANA 607, fuselage sides - Intermediate Blue ANA 608, wing and tail uppersurfaces - Semi-Gloss Sea Blue ANA 606 and under surfaces Insignia White ANA 601.*

SBD-5 *of VS-37, Atlantic Fleet, February 1944, Anti-Submarine duties (ASW).*
The Atlantic ASW camouflage was Dark Gull Gray uppersurfaces and Insignia White undersurfaces.

SBD-5 *of Bombing 16 (VB-16) on USS Lexington (CV 16), June 1944. Flown by Lt Cook Cleland and Radioman 2nd Class William J. Hisler.*

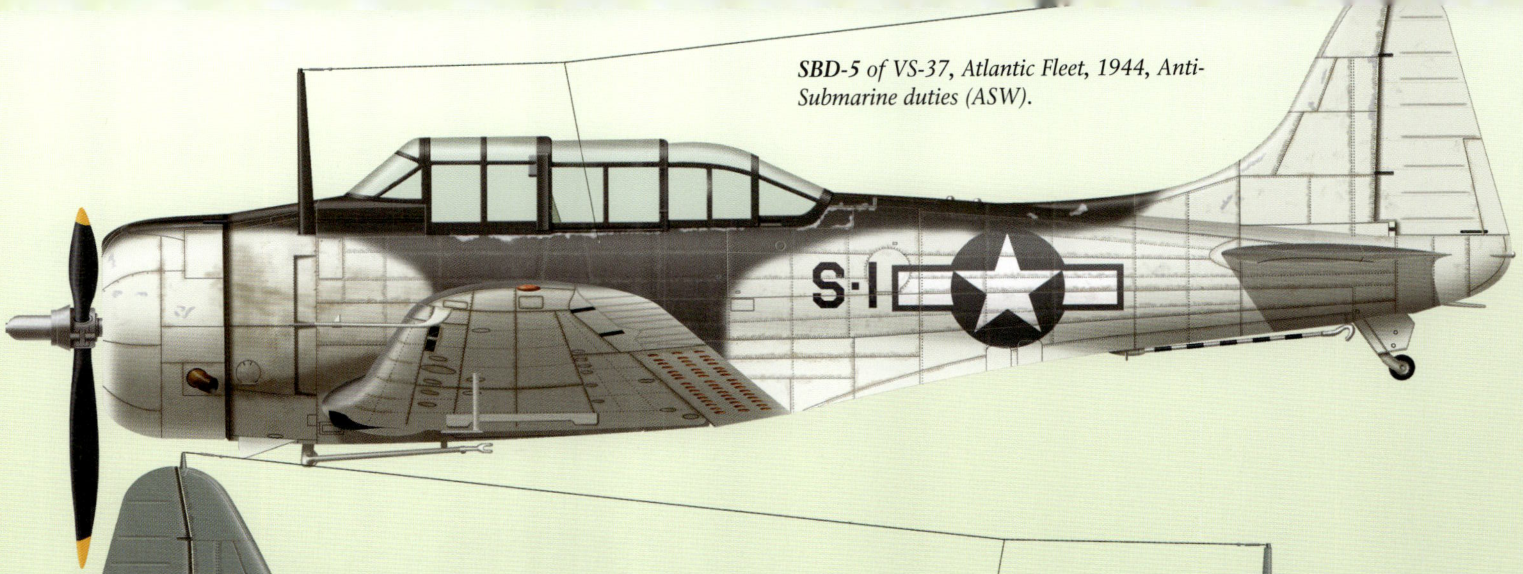

SBD-5 *of VS-37, Atlantic Fleet, 1944, Anti-Submarine duties (ASW).*

SBD-4 *of Marine Air Group 14, RNZAF, Seagrove, Auckland, July 1943. Aircraft still with US markings.*

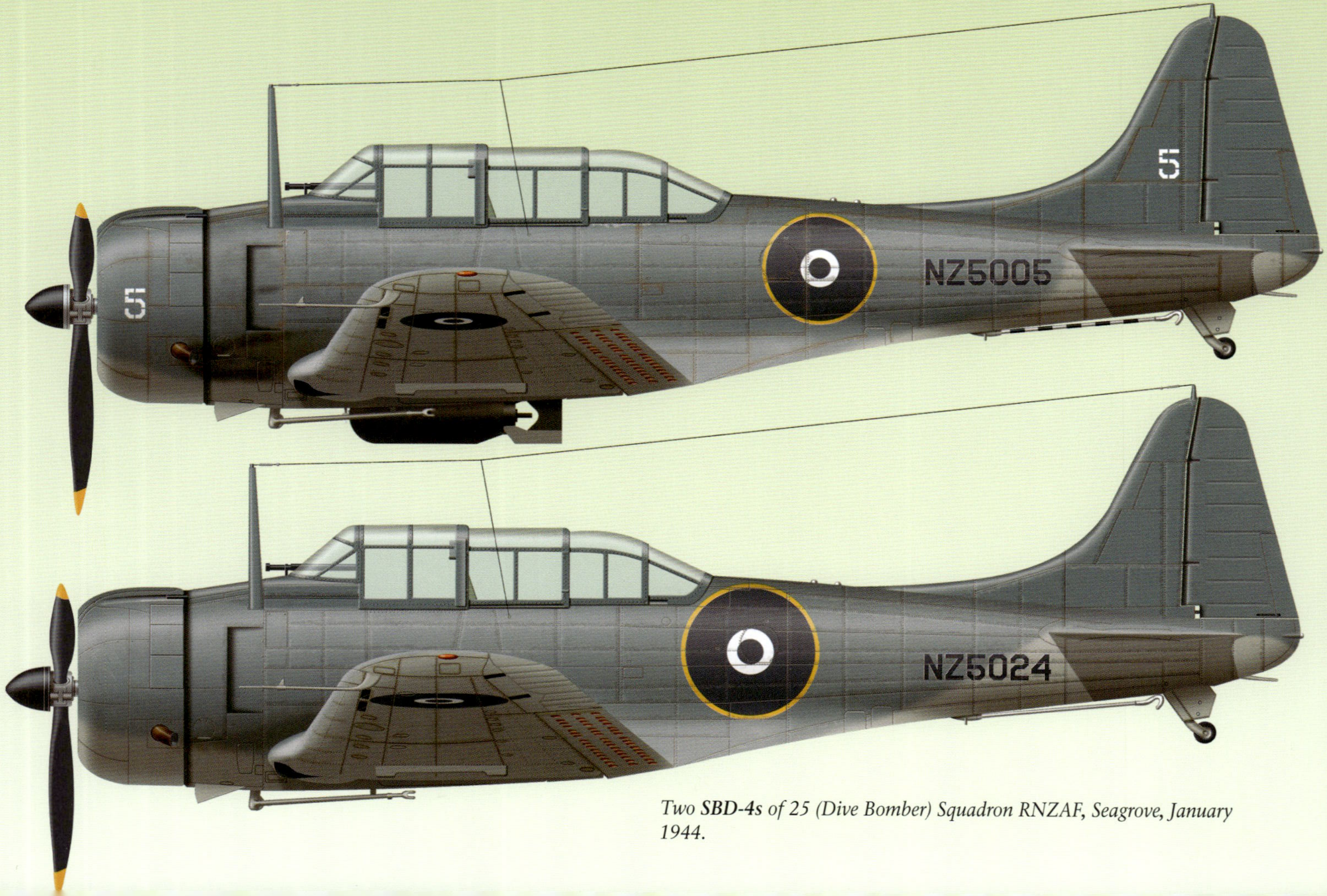

Two **SBD-4s** *of 25 (Dive Bomber) Squadron RNZAF, Seagrove, January 1944.*

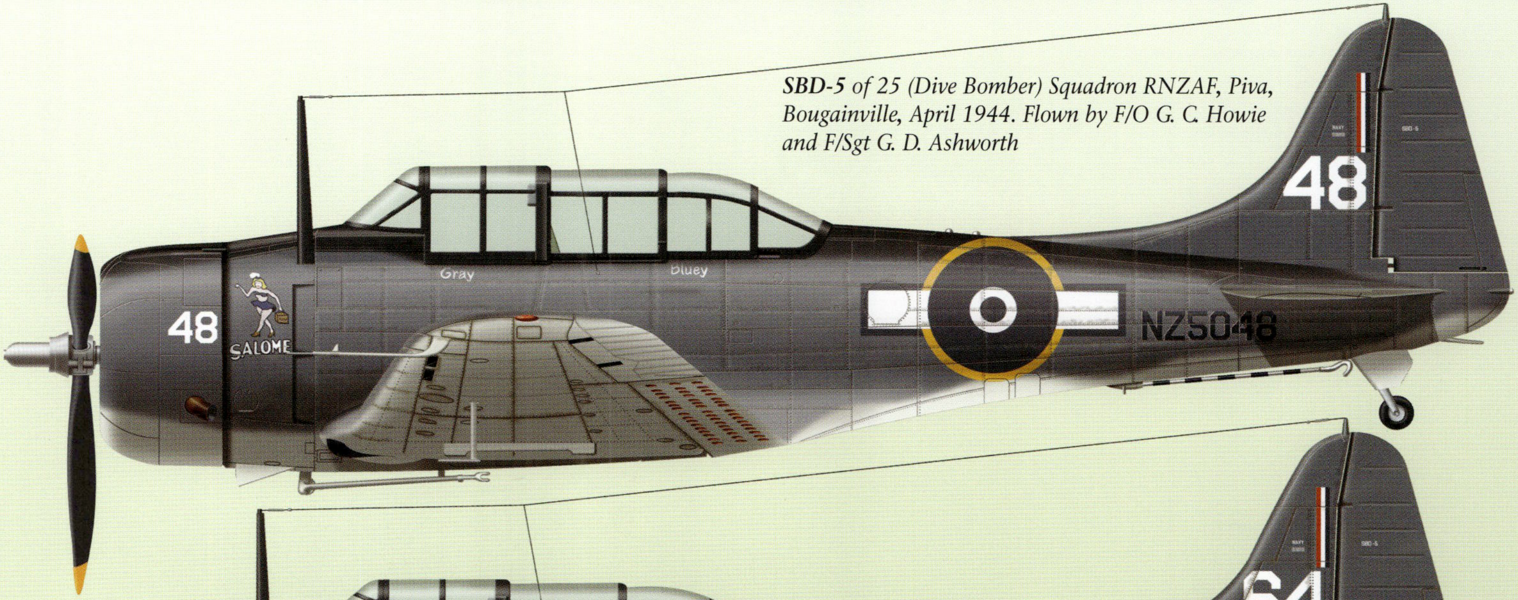

SBD-5 *of 25 (Dive Bomber) Squadron RNZAF, Piva, Bougainville, April 1944. Flown by F/O G. C. Howie and F/Sgt G. D. Ashworth*

SBD-5 *of 25 (Dive Bomber) Squadron RNZAF, Piva, Bougainville, April 1944. Flown by F/O B. N. Graham and F/Sgt. O. E. Watson*

A-24B *of Groupe de combat I/18 "Vendee", France, 1944.*
Standard US Air Force camouflage, Olive Drab uppersurfaces and Neutral Gray under surfaces.

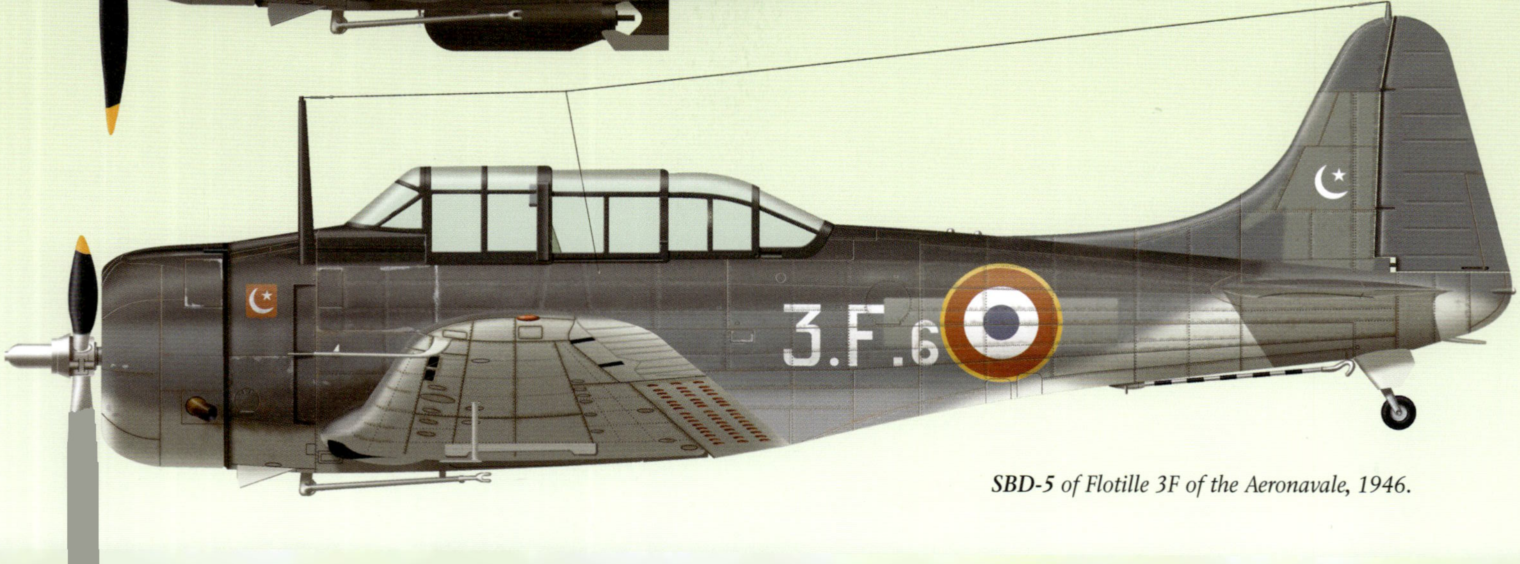

SBD-5 *of Flotille 3F of the Aeronavale, 1946.*

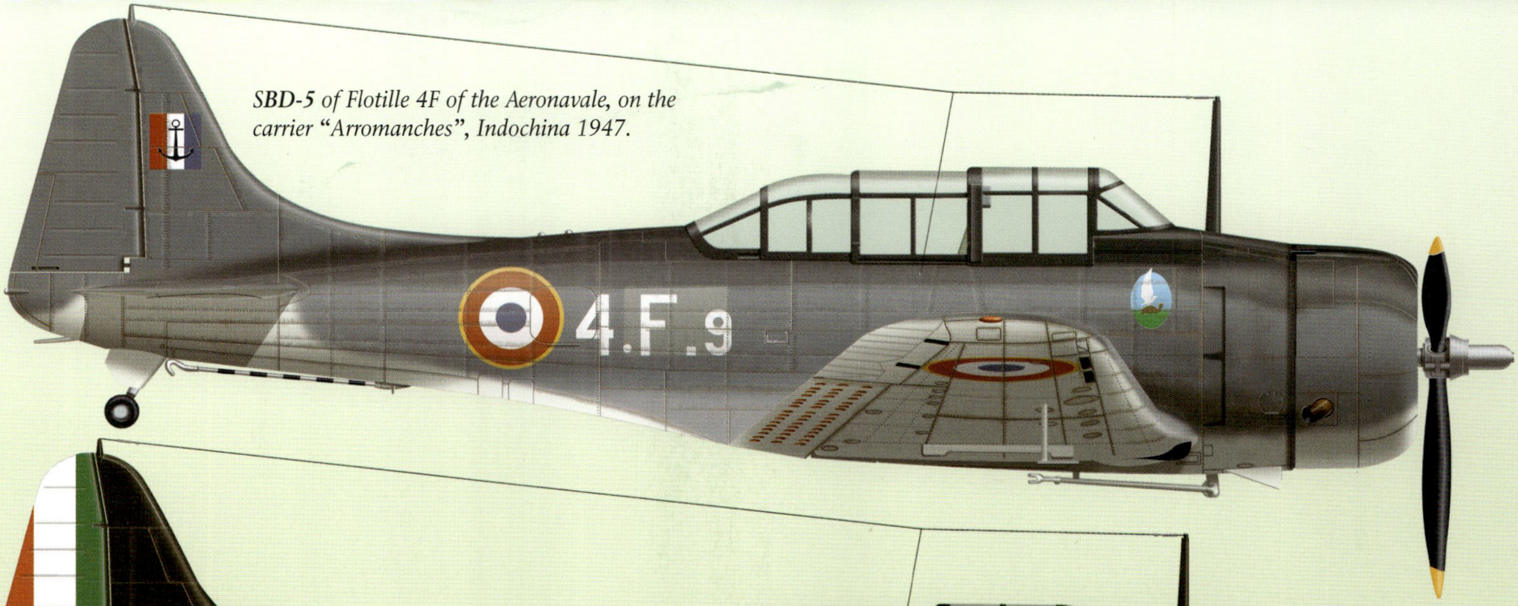

SBD-5 *of Flotille 4F of the Aeronavale, on the carrier "Arromanches", Indochina 1947.*

A-24 *of Fuerza Aerea Mexicana (Mexican Air Force), 1945. Aircraft in standard US Air Force camouflage.*

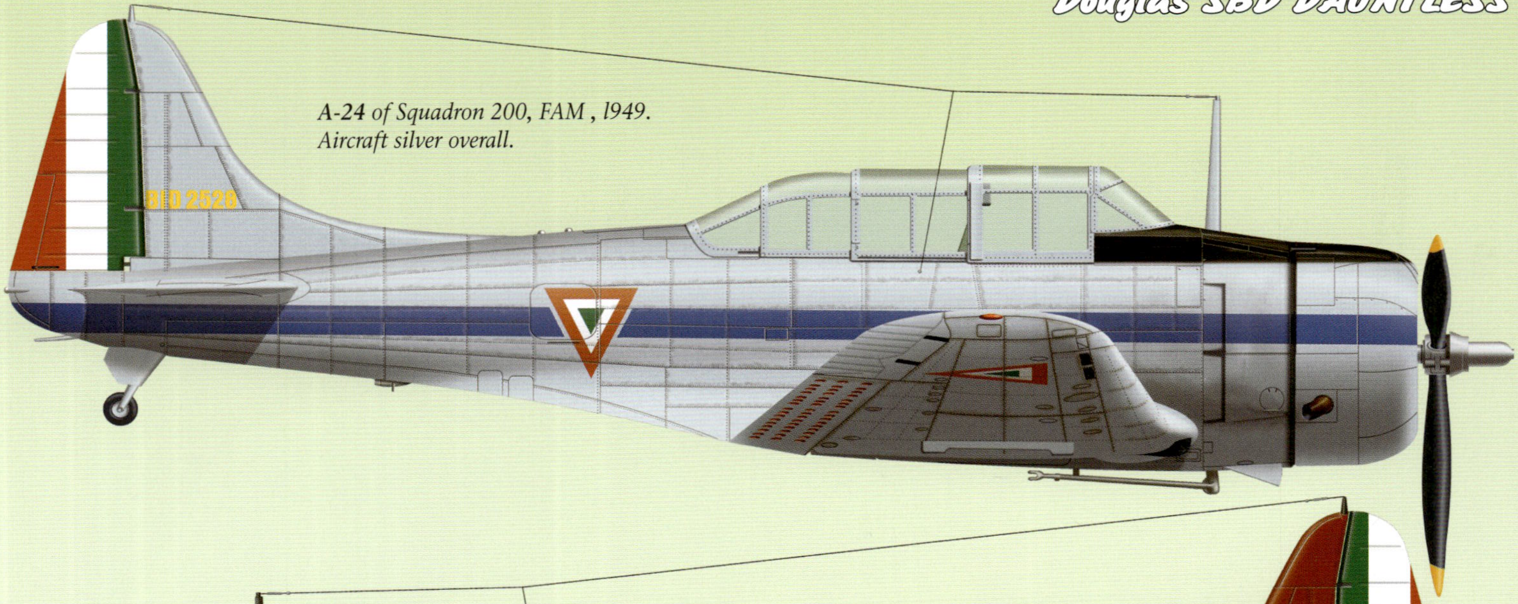

A-24 *of Squadron 200, FAM , 1949.*
Aircraft silver overall.

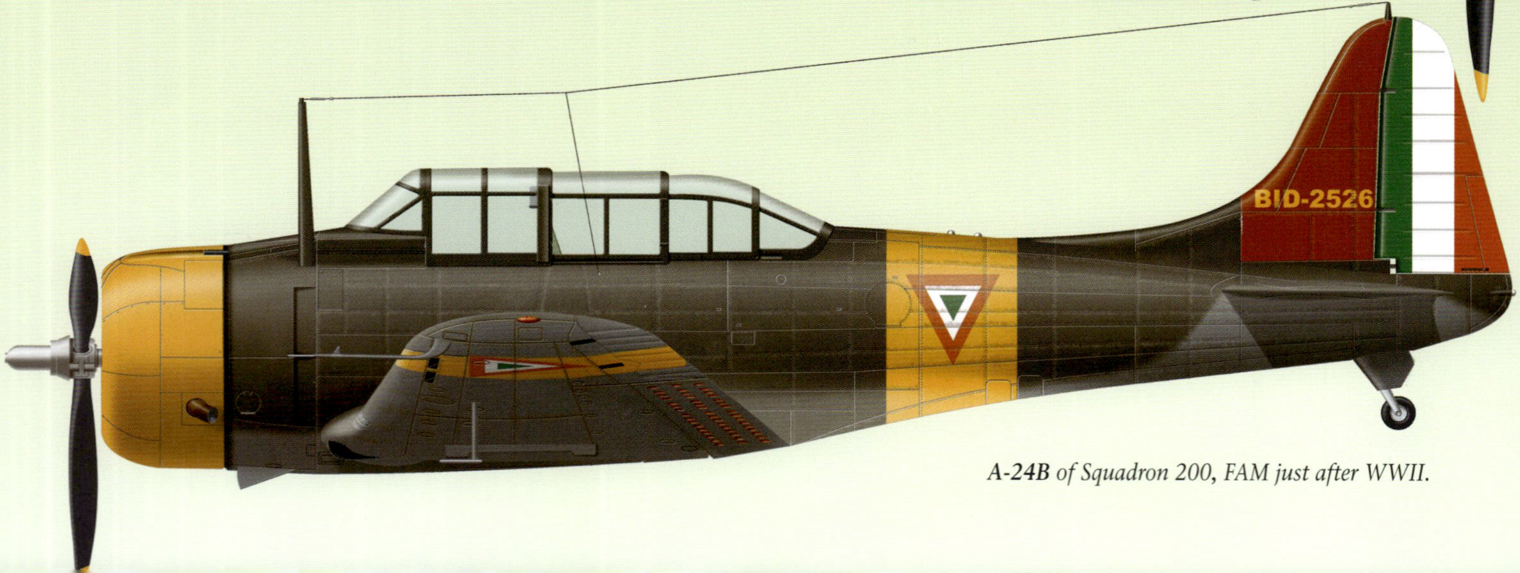

A-24B *of Squadron 200, FAM just after WWII.*

A-24 of Cia-Mes-Aerofoto SA, late '50s.

SBD-5 *used by Mexican pilots at USN air station on North Island, San Diego, 1944.*

***A-24** with FACh no 712, 1950. Personal aircraft of Commander in Chief of Flight.*

A-24 with FACh no 709, late '40s.

A-24B-1-DT, S/N 42-54298 "Bar Fly"

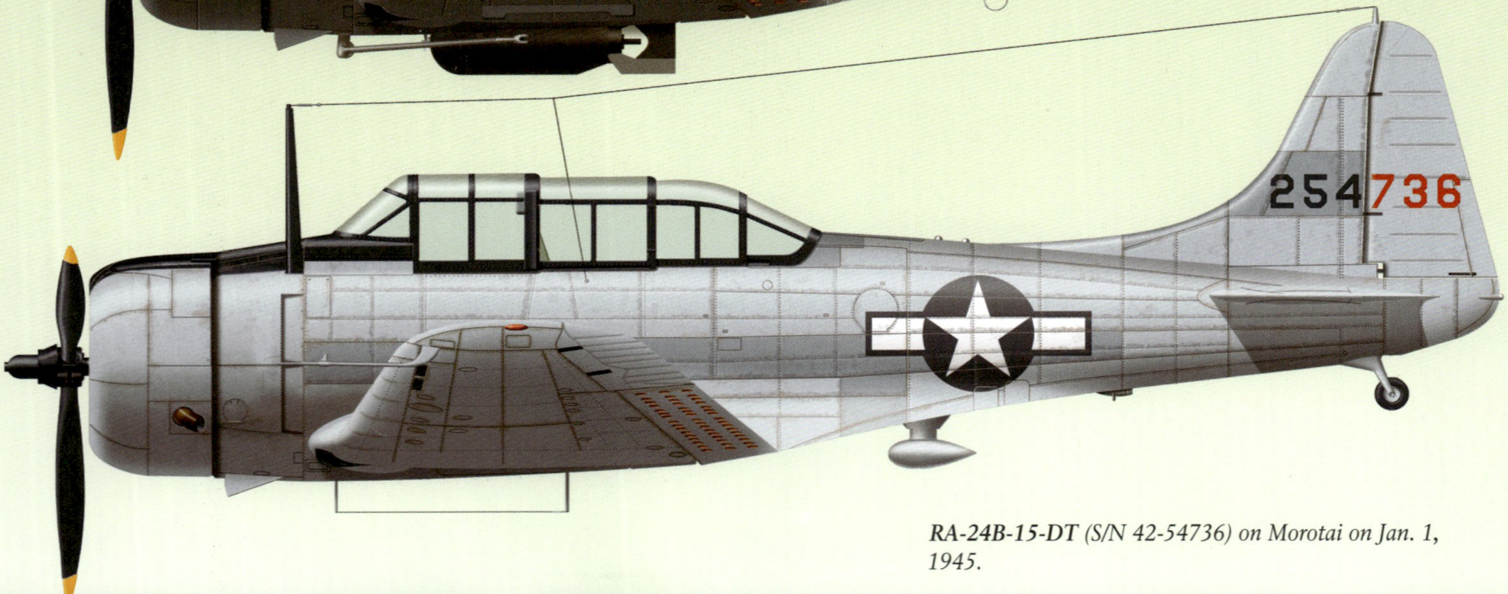

RA-24B-15-DT *(S/N 42-54736) on Morotai on Jan. 1, 1945.*